50 CHINESE COFFEE BREAKS

SHORT ACTIVITIES TO IMPROVE YOUR MANDARIN CHINESE ONE CUP AT A TIME

COFFEE BREAK LANGUAGES

Activities developed by

顾利程 LICHENG GU

Introduction by

MARK PENTLETON

Series Editor

AVA DINWOODIE

CoffeeBreak
Chinese

First published by Teach Yourself in 2026
An imprint of John Murray Press

I

A CIP catalogue record for this title is available from the British Library

Paperback ISBN 9781399823357
ebook ISBN 9781399823364

Typeset by KnowledgeWorks Global Ltd.

Printed and bound in Great Britain by Clays Ltd, Elcograf S.p.A.

John Murray Press policy is to use papers that are natural, renewable and recyclable products and made from wood grown in sustainable forests. The logging and manufacturing processes are expected to conform to the environmental regulations of the country of origin.

John Murray Press
Carmelite House
50 Victoria Embankment
London EC4Y 0DZ

Teach Yourself
Hachette Book Group
123 South Broad Street
Ste 2750
Philadelphia, PA 19109, USA

www.teachyourself.com

John Murray Press, part of Hodder & Stoughton Limited
An Hachette UK company

The authorised representative in the EEA is Hachette Ireland,
8 Castlecourt Centre, Dublin 15, D15 XTP3, Ireland (email: info@hbgi.ie)

CONTENTS

来一杯咖啡吗?
Lái yì bēi kāfēi ma?

来一杯咖啡吗? **Lái yì bēi kāfēi ma?** Fancy a coffee? This book is designed to make it easy for you to learn just a little bit of Chinese every single time you take a Coffee Break.

It is divided into three sections, so that you can decide how long you've got and choose an activity that will fill whatever time you have. Is it just a quick espresso? A little longer for an americano or a latte? Whether you have 5, 10 or 15 minutes for your Coffee Break today, we have something to accompany your refreshment.

Throughout the book you will find a variety of activities, including reading texts, grammar exercises, writing tasks, idiom explanations and vocabulary practice.

Simply decide how long you have, choose an activity from the 5-, 10- or 15-minute Coffee Break section and start learning. 我们开始吧! **Wǒmen kāishǐ ba!**

ABOUT COFFEE BREAK LANGUAGES

Coffee Break Languages came into being in 2006 with the launch of the Coffee Break Spanish podcast. As the first podcast for beginners in Spanish, the idea of "learning a language on your coffee break" quickly took off, and soon learners around the world were using the Coffee Break Languages podcasts and online courses to build their language skills.

Since then the Coffee Break method has grown to cover 10 languages and has been recognised through numerous awards, including European Professional Podcast of the Year and the European Award for Languages.

The Coffee Break Languages team of language experts, teachers and native speakers is led by Mark Pentleton. A former high school languages teacher himself, Mark continues to share his passion for language learning, and the opportunities it provides, with learners around the world through podcasts, videos, courses and books.

INTRODUCTION
THE IMPORTANCE OF PRACTICE

MARK PENTLETON

"You've got to learn your instrument. Then you practise, practise, practise."

It was the virtuoso jazz saxophonist Charlie Parker who outlined the importance of practice in this way. Indeed, in a 1954 interview with fellow musician Paul Desmond, he explained that, over the course of three or four years, he would spend up to 15 hours a day practising. This allowed him to master the improvisation skills which then led to the development of bebop and influenced countless musicians who came after him.

No matter what skill you are acquiring, regular practice plays a crucial part. And don't worry, we're not suggesting 15 hours a day! You may well bake several hundred croissants before becoming confident in your ability to master the recipe. If you're doing the Couch to 5K running plan, you need to train regularly before you're ready to tackle those 5,000 metres. And if your child happens to be learning to play the violin, then the old adage of "practice makes perfect" is probably something you say on a daily basis.

Your "instrument" is the Chinese language. You can already play some notes on the instrument, and perhaps you can even manage a few tunes. You're probably at the stage now of wanting to "perform" these tunes, using the Chinese you know in spoken and written situations, and perhaps even moving on to more complex pieces. But before you reach this stage, there's something you must do. You've guessed it: practise!

As I said, there's no need to follow the same intense practice schedule as Charlie Parker, spending many hours a day on your language skills. Indeed, since our very first Coffee Break Languages lesson back in 2006, we've stressed the importance of "little and often" when it comes to improving your language skills. And that's exactly what this book is about.

We've brought together a collection of interesting and enjoyable exercises which will help you build your vocabulary, increase your understanding of grammar and develop a cultural awareness, all within the space of a "coffee break".

Through the exercises, you'll learn new words, see examples of grammar points that you know and learn new constructions. You'll complete reading challenges, acquire new idiomatic expressions and learn to describe what you see in a photo, a skill which you can take into your daily life and use to practise your language wherever and whenever you want.

If you're training for a marathon, there's no doubt that the practice you put in beforehand is hard work. But language learning is not a marathon: it's a stroll in the park, a walk along a beach at sunset, or a drive along a beautiful lakeside as the early-morning mist clears. By ensuring that your practice is enjoyable, you'll make faster progress and you'll benefit from deeper learning. And that's exactly why we've written this book of fun and engaging exercises.

I started the introduction to this book with a quotation by Charlie Parker. However, I didn't give the full quotation. Having established the fact that, after learning the basics, what you need to do to master an instrument is "practise, practise, practise", Charlie Parker went on to add a third stage in this process:

> "And then, when you finally get up there on the bandstand, forget all that and just wail."

That, in a sense, is what we're all aiming for as language learners. Of course, "wailing" may sound unpleasant and conjure up images of tears and despair, but in the context of jazz music, Parker was suggesting that if you've learned the tune and practised over and over again, then you are ready to fly, enjoying the moment and letting the music flow naturally. When you have completed all the exercises in this book, I hope you feel ready to "fly", "wail" or simply enjoy the moment, letting your language flow naturally using the new words, phrases and grammar points you've practised.

So, all you need to do now is decide how long you'd like to spend on your Chinese today, pick any of our Coffee Break-length exercises, and begin your practice. I wish you "happy language learning" and, of course, "happy coffee breaking"!

HOW TO USE THIS BOOK

The activities in this book vary slightly in their difficulty from one to the next, but are generally around lower intermediate level, or A2–B1 on the CEFR. Remember that even if you find a particular activity a little easier, consolidation is a vital part of language learning and no learning is ever wasted.

CHINESE CHARACTERS AND PINYIN

The activities in the book are written in Chinese characters with the support of pinyin. In this way, the book is designed to help you practise your Mandarin Chinese in whatever way is appropriate and useful for your level and learning focus.

In most activities we provide the Chinese characters first, followed by the pinyin. In some activities, which feature a longer passage in Chinese, we have chosen to include pinyin above the characters to help you build your confidence in reading characters.

If improving your recognition and writing of Chinese characters is part of your learning, we'd encourage you to focus on the characters, rather than the pinyin, and where you're invited to write in Chinese, have a go at writing the characters. If your focus is solely on spoken Chinese, however, you can use the pinyin to help you read, and when it comes to writing exercises, you can write in pinyin. Of course, if you're somewhere in between, you can find the balance that works best for you.

Both Chinese characters and pinyin will be provided in the answers section, where relevant.

WRITING

✎ This pencil icon followed by a line indicates a space for you to write your answers, but feel free to add your own notes in any blank spaces on the pages too.

CHECKLISTS

At the start of every section of the book you have a checklist, where you can record your Coffee Breaks by ticking off activities as you complete them.

ANSWERS SECTIONS

At the end of each activity, we'll tell you which page to turn to if there is an answers section. Take your time to read the examples and explanations that we give you. If there are words or phrases that are new for you, remember to use your dictionary to help you. You can use any space on the page or your own notebook to write this new vocabulary and help you remember it. There is also some extra space at the back of this book where you can write notes.

TYPES OF ACTIVITY

Each of the three sections of this book contains a number of different types of activity. Below, you'll find a description of each type, so that you know what to expect every time you choose an activity. Whether you're looking for some reading practice, a writing task, some help with grammar or something else, we hope that these descriptions help you to decide how you're going to spend each Coffee Break.

5-MINUTE COFFEE BREAKS

Word Builder

In these activities, you will learn some interesting pieces of vocabulary on a variety of topics. There is then a short exercise to allow you to practise this vocabulary in context. To make the most of the Word Builder activities, we recommend writing down the words that are new to you in your own notes to help you remember them.

Mini Grammar Challenge

These challenges are designed to give you a little extra practice on some tricky Chinese grammar points. Each activity will focus on one specific point and will include a brief explanation, an exercise and answers.

Idiomatically Speaking

In each of these activities, we will focus on one Chinese idiomatic expression. First, we will explain its meaning and give examples of some of the contexts in which the idiom can be used. Then, there will be a short exercise or space for you to practise using the idiom in your own sentences.

Say What You See

In these writing activities, we will provide some suggested phrases to help you write a description of an image. As there is no set answer for this type of exercise, you may not know whether what you've written is entirely correct. Don't worry about this too much, however, as the purpose of these writing activities is simply to get you writing freely in Chinese, practising creating different types of texts and, in this way, developing your writing skills. For these activities, we have included our own "answer", which we hope you will find useful. However, it's important to remember that there is no single correct answer, so don't worry if your description is very different. The possible "answer" we provide will be in both Chinese characters and pinyin, so however you've chosen to write your description, you'll have something to compare it to.

Guided Translation

Each of these activities is based on a short piece of text in Chinese: a famous quotation or a saying. We will talk you through the language used in the piece of text to examine in detail the vocabulary and structures used and to help you come up with a good translation.

10-MINUTE COFFEE BREAKS

Translation Challenge

In these activities, your challenge is to translate sentences from English into Chinese. There will be hints to help you, if you need them, and suggested translations and language explanations in the answers section. You can write in Chinese characters, pinyin or a mixture of the two, according to what is most appropriate for your level.

Famous Chinese Speakers

These are designed to help you develop both your reading skills and your cultural knowledge. They are based on texts about famous speakers of Chinese and include a vocabulary list and questions to help you test your understanding of the text.

For Good Measure

Mandarin Chinese has hundreds of measure words. You may also know these as counters or classifiers, and they are used alongside numbers to count items. Each of these activities will focus on a specific group of measure words to help you practise choosing which measure word to use and when to use it.

Number Focus

It takes a while, when learning a language, to reach the stage where you can instantly visualise the corresponding digit when you hear a number being said out loud. This can only become easier with practice, which is why our Number Focus activities include a variety of exercises designed to help you practise your numbers in Chinese.

Taste Bud Tantaliser

These activities use recipes as reading texts and include a vocabulary list and a reading comprehension exercise, so that you can practise your language skills while learning about a typical Chinese dish. While the activity should only take around 10 minutes, there's nothing stopping you from getting to know the language in the recipe even better by following it and making the dish yourself when you have more time!

15-MINUTE COFFEE BREAKS

Reading Focus

These longer reading activities will allow you to study a short text about a particular aspect of Chinese culture. They include a vocabulary list, comprehension questions and language questions.

Grammar Focus

While the 5-minute Mini Grammar Challenges are perfect for a short bit of practice of specific grammar points, in these Grammar Focus activities, we take a more in-depth look at different topics in Chinese grammar, providing more detailed explanations and a number of different exercises to help you practise.

Vocabulary Consolidation

This is a vocabulary drill exercise that will help you familiarise yourself with pieces of vocabulary on a specific topic. Each activity focuses on 20 pieces of vocabulary and includes a number of different exercises to help you practise and get to know them.

5-MINUTE COFFEE BREAKS

CHECKLIST
5-MINUTE COFFEE BREAKS

Word Builder

Mini Grammar Challenge

Idiomatically Speaking

Say What You See

Guided Translation

1

城市生活
Chéngshì shēnghuó
WORD BUILDER

In this Word Builder, we're focusing on a few essential reference points to help you find your way in a Chinese-speaking city. Read through the vocabulary list below and note down the words that are new to you to help you remember them. Then, complete the exercise that follows to practise using them.

* * *

商店 shāngdiàn	*shop, store*
医院 yīyuàn	*hospital*
动物园 dòngwùyuán	*zoo*
饭馆 fànguǎn	*restaurant*
汽车站 qìchēzhàn	*bus stop*
银行 yínháng	*bank*
地铁站 dìtiě zhàn	*subway station*
厕所 cèsuǒ	*toilet, washroom*

Now, let's practise using this vocabulary in context. Fill in the gaps in the following sentences with the most appropriate piece of vocabulary from the list.

1. 我不舒服。请带我去 ✎＿＿＿＿＿＿＿＿＿＿＿＿ 。
   Wǒ bù shūfu. Qǐng dài wǒ qù ✎＿＿＿＿＿＿＿＿＿＿＿＿.

2. 我要坐地铁。请问，✎＿＿＿＿＿＿＿＿＿＿＿＿
   怎么走？ **Wǒ yào zuò dìtiě. Qǐngwèn,**
   ✎＿＿＿＿＿＿＿＿＿＿＿＿ **zěnme zǒu?**

3. 我要买水，哪里有 ✎＿＿＿＿＿＿＿＿＿＿＿＿？
   Wǒ yào mǎi shuǐ. Nǎlǐ yǒu ✎＿＿＿＿＿＿＿＿＿＿＿＿?

4. 我要坐车，附近有 ✎＿＿＿＿＿＿＿＿＿＿＿＿ 吗？
   Wǒ yào zuòchē, fùjìn yǒu ✎＿＿＿＿＿＿＿＿＿＿＿＿
   ma?

5. 我还没有看见过大熊猫，我们今天去
   ✎＿＿＿＿＿＿＿＿＿＿＿＿ 吧。 **Wǒ hái méi yǒu**
   kànjiàn guò dàxióngmāo, wǒmen jīntiān qù
   ✎＿＿＿＿＿＿＿＿＿＿＿＿ **ba.**

* * *

Once you're happy with your answers, turn to pages 63-64 to check them.

2

怎么用"了"
Zěnme yòng "le"
MINI GRAMMAR CHALLENGE

In this Mini Grammar Challenge, we're going to focus on the use of
了 le. Read the explanation below, then put your knowledge to the
test in the exercise that follows. Good luck!

* * *

To indicate the completion of an action, 了 le is placed at the end of
the sentence. Let's compare the following two sentences:

Wǒ jīntiān kàn shū.
我今天看书。   *I am reading books today.*

Wǒ jīntiān kàn shū le.
我今天看书了。   *I have read books today.*

In the above examples, 我今天看书 **wǒ jīntiān kàn shū** simply
means that I plan to read books today, while 我今天看书了

wǒ jīntiān kàn shū le means I have completed the task of reading for the day. Let's look at a couple more examples:

Wǒ shàngwǔ dǎqiú le.

我上午打球了。 *I played ball in the morning.*

Wǒ chī wǔfàn le.

我吃午饭了。 *I ate my lunch.*

EXERCISE

Rewrite the following sentences and change the habitual or future actions into completed actions by putting 了 **le** at the end of the sentence. Then, try translating the sentences into English.

1. 他喝茶。 **Tā hē chá.**

   ✎_____

   _____

2. 她哥哥写毛笔字。 **Tā gēge xiě máobǐzì.**

   ✎_____

   _____

3. 我妈妈今天做鱼。 **Wǒ māma jīntiān zuò yú.**

   ✎_____

   _____

4. 姐姐在家洗衣服。 **Jiějie zàijiā xǐ yīfu.**

   ✎_____

   _____

5. 妹妹今天游泳。　**Mèimei jīntiān yóuyǒng.**

✎_____

_____

* * *

When you're ready, the answers can be found on page 64.

3

一石二鸟
Yī shí èr niǎo
IDIOMATICALLY SPEAKING

The focus of this activity is the idiomatic expression 一石二鸟 **yī shí èr niǎo**. The word-for-word translation of this Chinese idiom is *one stone, two birds*. As you can probably guess, the English equivalent is *to kill two birds with one stone*; the idiom is almost exactly the same in the two languages. Let's take a look at some examples of this expression in context:

Qí zìxíngchē qù shàngbān, jì kěyǐ jiǎnshǎo wūrǎn, yòu kěyǐ duànliàn shēntǐ, zhēn shì yī shí èr niǎo a.
骑自行车去上班, 既可以减少污染, 又可以锻炼身体, 真是一石二鸟啊。
Going to work by bike can not only reduce pollution but also allow you to exercise. It really does kill two birds with one stone.

Qù Zhōngguó lǚyóu? Zhè zhēn shì yí ge yī shí èr niǎo de hǎo zhúyi. Búdàn kěyǐ chī dìdào de Zhōngguó fàn, érqiě kěyǐ xué dìdào de Zhōngwén.

去中国旅游？这真是一个一石二鸟的好主意。不但可以吃地道的中国饭，而且可以学地道的中文。

Travelling around China? This is a great idea that will kill two birds with one stone. Not only can you eat authentic Chinese food, but you can also learn authentic Chinese.

Nǐ qù yínháng de lùshang shùnbiàn bāng wǒ bǎ shū huán dào túshūguǎn, búshì yī shí èr niǎo ma?

你去银行的路上顺便帮我把书还到图书馆，不是一石二鸟吗？

On your way to the bank, return the book to the library for me. Doesn't that kill two birds with one stone?

Can you come up with a few of your own examples? Use the lines below to write three of your own sentences containing this idiom. Write in Chinese characters, pinyin or a mixture of the two – whatever helps you practise Chinese in the way you're learning.

✎_____

_____

_____

_____

_____

_____

_____

_____

_____

_____

_____

_____

_____

_____

4

年夜饭
Niányèfàn

SAY WHAT YOU SEE

How would you describe what's going on in this photo? Use the suggested phrases and vocabulary on the next page to help you write three to five sentences describing the scene. You can choose to write in Chinese characters, pinyin or a mixture of the two. 加油! Jiāyóu!

SUGGESTED PHRASES

正在吃 **zhèngzài chī**	*to be eating*
厨房 **chúfáng**	*kitchen*
年夜饭 **niányèfàn**	*New Year's dinner*
桌子周围坐着* **zhuōzi zhōuwéi zuò zhe**	*around the table sit*
小女孩 **xiǎo nǚhái**	*little girl*
左边坐着 **zuǒbiān zuò zhe**	*is sitting on the left*
爷爷 **yéye**	*paternal grandfather*
姥爷 **lǎoye**	*maternal grandfather*
奶奶 **nǎinai**	*paternal grandmother*
姥姥 **lǎolao**	*maternal grandmother*
前面摆着 **qiánmiàn bǎi zhe**	*at the front there is / are*
碗 **wǎn**	*bowl*
盘子 **pánzi**	*plate*
筷子 **kuàizi**	*chopsticks*
桌子中间摆着 **zhuōzi zhōngjiān bǎi zhe**	*in the middle of the table there is / are*
其中有 **qízhōng yǒu**	*among them are*
火锅 **huǒguō**	*hot pot*
鱼 **yú**	*fish*
肉 **ròu**	*meat*
蘑菇 **mógu**	*mushroom*
各种青菜 **gèzhǒng qīngcài**	*all kinds of green vegetables*

墙上挂着 **qiángshang guàzhe** *is hanging on the wall*

铲子 **chǎnzi** *spatula*

勺子 **sháozi** *ladle*

灯笼 **dēnglong** *lantern*

(正)在碰杯 **(zhèng)zài pèngbēi** *to be clinking glasses*

新年快乐! **Xīnnián kuàilè!** *Happy New Year!*

*To help you describe the scene, you may find the following structure useful: *location + verb* + 着 **zhe** + *topic*. This structure is explained in a Mini Grammar Challenge on page 36.

_____

_____

_____

_____

_____

_____

_____

_____

_____

_____

_____

_____

_____

_____

_____

_____

* * *

If you'd like to see what we came up with, turn to page 65.

5

三人行，必有我师

Sān rén xíng, bì yǒu wǒ shī

GUIDED TRANSLATION

Confucius (孔子 **Kǒngzǐ**) was a Chinese philosopher whose ideas and teachings have influenced Chinese culture and many other societies around the world. In this Guided Translation, we're going to look at one of his famous sayings, word by word, in order to understand the message it conveys.

三人行，必有我师。　**Sān rén xíng, bì yǒu wǒ shī.**

LANGUAGE EXPLANATION

Let's take a closer look at the language used in this quotation.

We'll begin with 三人 **sān rén**. You'll recognise the three lines in 三 **sān**, which make up the character for the number *three*.

The next one will also be familiar to you, as it is the very commonly used character 人 **rén** for *person* or *people*.

The third character, 行 **xíng**, is a verb. It is abbreviated from 行走 **xíngzǒu**.

Now, let's look at the next four characters. 必 **bì** is short for 必定 **bìdìng**, meaning *surely*. 有 **yǒu** means *to have* or *there is / are*.

The last word, 师 **shī**, comes from 老师 **lǎoshī**, which means *teacher* or *to learn from*. Here, 我师 **wǒ shī** could mean *my teacher* or *for me to learn from*.

Now, try putting all this together to figure out the meaning of this Confucius quotation. Good luck!

✎_____

_____

_____

* * *

When you think you know the meaning, turn to page 66 to find the answer.

6

三点水和两点水
Sāndiǎnshuǐ hé liǎngdiǎnshuǐ
WORD BUILDER

Our focus for this vocabulary activity is on how to build your Chinese vocabulary with the help of radicals. A radical, or indexing component, is a visually prominent component of a category of characters that share a similar meaning. In this activity, we are going to focus on Chinese characters that include the "water" radical 氵 or the "ice" radical 冫 and explore their meaning. You can see that the water radical has two falling dots and one rising dot, while the ice radical has only one falling dot and one rising dot. The characters that have the 氵 radical are all related to liquid, while the characters that have the 冫 radical are all related to ice.

* * *

Let's see some characters that have the water radical:

河 **hé**   *river*
游 **yóu**   *swim*

汤 tāng   *soup*

汗 hàn   *sweat*

Now let's look at some characters that have the ice radical:

冰 bīng   *ice*

冻 dòng   *frozen*

凋 diāo   *withered*

凌 líng   *sleet*

From these examples, you can see that radicals help to reveal the meaning of the characters. By understanding the function of radicals, you can often guess the meaning of a character even if it is new to you.

EXERCISE

Now, let's see if you can figure out which radical – water 氵 or ice 冫 – to add to the left of the following characters. Then, write the whole character in the box to match the English translation. We've done the first one for you:

e.g. 由 [油] *oil*

1. 令   *chilly*

2. 目   *tears*

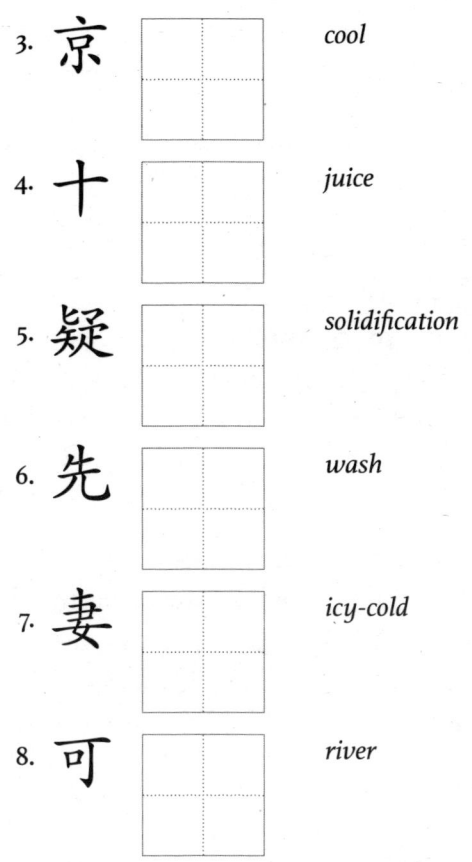

3. 京   *cool*

4. 十   *juice*

5. 疑   *solidification*

6. 先   *wash*

7. 妻   *icy-cold*

8. 可   *river*

* * *

你真棒! **Nǐ zhēn bàng!** When you've finished adding the radicals, check your answers on page 66.

怎么用"着"1
Zěnme yòng "zhe" 1
MINI GRAMMAR CHALLENGE

In this activity, we're going to practise using 着 zhe following a verb to describe what you see, especially when you want to illustrate the current state or condition that someone is in. You use the *verb* + 着 zhe structure to provide a description rather than to report the action that someone is carrying out. 祝你成功! Zhù nǐ chénggōng!

***

Let's compare the following pair of sentences:

Māma yídìng yào xiǎohái chuān báisè de yīfu.
妈妈一定要小孩穿白色的衣服。

The mother insisted that her child wear white clothes.

Zhàopiān lǐ de xiǎohái chuān zhe báisè de yīfu.
照片里的小孩穿着白色的衣服。

The child in the photo is in white clothes.

In the first sentence, 穿 **chuān** means *to wear* or *to put on*. However, if we add 着 **zhe** right after the verb, as in the second sentence, it means *to be wearing* or *to be in*.

With 着 **zhe** after a verb, the sentence changes from an action to a description of what you see.

EXERCISE 1

Decide which is the correct translation of each English sentence and circle either A or B.

1. *All the people who came in were wearing black clothes.*
   A. 进来的人都穿黑色的衣服。
   B. 进来的人都穿着黑色的衣服。

2. *The man left. He was wearing a striped T-shirt.*
   A. 那个人走了。他穿条纹上衣。
   B. 那个人走了。他穿着条纹上衣。

3. *The person in the middle is wearing a red overcoat.*
   A. 中间那个人穿着红色的大衣。
   B. 中间那个人穿红色的大衣。

USING 戴着 dài zhe

The verb 戴 **dài** also means *to wear*, but it refers to wearing accessories like a hat, watch, badge, scarf or gloves. For example, 请戴帽子 **qǐng dài màozi** means *please put on a hat*. As in the previous examples, if we add 着 **zhe** after the verb 戴 **dài**, it means *to be wearing a hat*. Let's look at two more examples:

Wūzi lǐ de rén dōu dài zhe màozi.

屋子里的人都戴着帽子。

All the people in the room are wearing hats.

Huà lǐ de rén dōu dài zhe shǒubiǎo.

画里的人都戴着手表。

All the people in the drawing are wearing watches.

EXERCISE 2

Now decide on the correct translation of the following sentences. Circle either A or B each time.

1. *The person on the left is wearing a pair of big glasses.*
   A. 左边那个人戴着一副大眼镜。
   B. 左边那个人戴一副大眼镜。

2. *Before you go out, please put on a hat.*
   A. 出门之前请戴着帽子。
   B. 出门之前请戴帽子。

3. *The little girl in the photo has a flower in her hair.*
   A. 照片里的小女孩头上戴着一朵花。
   B. 照片里的小女孩头上戴一朵花。

* * *

Once you're happy with your answers, you can check them on pages 66-67.

8

说一不二和朝三暮四
Shuō yī bú èr hé zhāo sān mù sì
IDIOMATICALLY SPEAKING

In this activity, we're looking at a pair of interesting idiomatic expressions in Chinese: 说一不二 **shuō yī bú èr** and 朝三暮四 **zhāo sān mù sì**. The word-for-word translation of the idiom 说一不二 **shuō yī bú èr** is *say one, not two*. If we think about this further, we can understand that the expression illustrates the simple fact that if someone says *one*, they mean *one* and not *two*. This idiom therefore conveys the idea of being true to your word or standing by a decision.

The second idiom, 朝三暮四 **zhāo sān mù sì**, literally means *morning three, dusk four*. The meaning of 朝三暮四 is the opposite of 说一不二. If in the morning you say *three* but in the evening you say *four*, you don't stick to your word and you often change your mind.

Let's look at some examples of these two expressions in context:

Tā shì yí ge shuō yī bú èr de rén. Shuō chūlái de huà cónglái bù shōuhuí.

他是一个说一不二的人。说出来的话从来不收回。

He is a man who means what he says. He never goes back on his word.

Wǒmen zuò shìqing bù néng zhāo sān mù sì de. Zuò chūlái de juédìng bù néng gǎi lái gǎi qù.

我们做事情不能朝三暮四的。做出来的决定不能改来改去。

We shouldn't keep changing our minds. We need to stick to the decisions we made.

Tā shì yí ge shuō yī bú èr de rén háishì yí ge zhāo sān mù sì de rén ne? Wǒ kàn tā shì yí ge zhāo sān mù sì de rén.

他是一个说一不二的人还是一个朝三暮四的人呢？
我看他是一个朝三暮四的人。

Is he a man of his word or a man who keeps changing his mind?
I think he is a man who keeps changing his mind.

Can you come up with a few of your own examples? Use the lines below to write three of your own sentences containing these idioms.

✎_____

_____

_____

_____

_____

_____

_____

_____

_____

_____

_____

_____

_____

_____

9

在公园
Zài gōngyuán
SAY WHAT YOU SEE

In this activity, we're focusing on writing skills. Take a close look at the image below, then use the suggested phrases on the next page to help you write a short description of the scene. 加油! **Jiāyóu!**

在公园

SUGGESTED PHRASES

这是在 zhè shì zài	*this is in*
公园里 gōngyuán lǐ	*in a park*
天气 tiānqì	*weather*
暖和 nuǎnhuo	*warm*
短衣 duǎnyī	*short-sleeved shirt, T-shirt*
短裤 duǎnkù	*shorts*
正在跑步 zhèngzài pǎobù	*to be running*
走步 zǒubù	*to go for a walk*
骑自行车 qí zìxíngchē	*to ride a bike*
左边 zuǒbiān	*on the left*
右边 yòubiān	*on the right*
中间 zhōngjiān	*in the middle*
一男一女 yì nán yì nǚ	*a man and a woman*
向…… 跑来 xiàng … pǎolái	*to run towards …*
聊天 liáotiān	*to chat*
一边……, 一边…… yìbiān … , yìbiān …	*to do … while doing …*
没有跑步 méi yǒu pǎobù	*is not running*
照看 zhàokàn	*to take care of*
婴儿车 yīng'érchē	*pram, stroller*
很可能 hěn kěnéng	*very likely*
小姑娘 xiǎo gūniáng	*little girl*
帮助 bāngzhù	*help*
姐姐 jiějie	*older sister*

两旁 liǎngpáng   *on both sides*

树 shù   *tree*

路灯 lùdēng   *streetlight*

在公园

_____

_____

_____

_____

_____

_____

_____

* * *

When you're ready, turn to pages 67-68 to see an example answer.

10

太阳从西边出来
Tàiyáng cóng xībiān chūlái
GUIDED TRANSLATION

Have you heard the witty saying 太阳从西边出来 **tàiyáng cóng xībiān chūlái**? In this Guided Translation, we're going to look at it word by word, in order to understand all the language used in it. As well as understanding the literal translation, it's important to know the meaning of the saying as a whole so that you fully understand when you hear it being used.

* * *

LANGUAGE EXPLANATION

We'll begin with 太阳 **tàiyáng**. These two characters mean *the sun*.

The third character, 从 **cóng**, means *from* or *in*.

西边 **xībiān** refers to the direction *west*.

The last two characters, 出来 **chūlái**, mean *to come out*.

Now, it's up to you to put all this together to figure out the meaning of this saying: 太阳从西边出来 tàiyáng cóng xībiān chūlái. You might be surprised by your translation!

✎_____

_____

_____

* * *

When you think you know the meaning, turn to pages 68-69 to find the translation and examples of the saying in context.

11

交通
Jiāotōng
WORD BUILDER

In this Word Builder, we're going to become more familiar with some of those all-important words that you'll need when you're next travelling in a Chinese-speaking area. Read through the vocabulary list, then have a go at the exercise that follows.

* * *

交通工具 jiāotōng gōngjù	*means of transport*
车票 chēpiào	*bus / train ticket*
船票 chuánpiào	*ship / boat / cruise ticket*
飞机票 fēijīpiào	*plane ticket*
站台 zhàntái	*platform*
登机口 dēngjīkǒu	*boarding gate*
站 zhàn	*stop, station*
换车 huànchē	*bus / train transfer*

转机 **zhuǎnjī**   *flight transfer*

接机 **jiējī**   *to pick somebody up at the airport*

送机 **sòngjī**   *to drop somebody off at the airport*

准点 **zhǔndiǎn**   *on time*

晚点 **wǎndiǎn**   *delayed*

Now it's over to you! On the lines below, describe one of your travel experiences. Try to include at least three of these pieces of vocabulary. Write in Chinese characters, pinyin or a mixture of the two – whatever helps you practise Chinese in the way you're learning. 祝你成功! **Zhù nǐ chénggōng!**

✎_____

_____

_____

_____

_____

_____

_____

_____

_____

_____

12

怎么用"着"2
Zěnme yòng "zhe" 2
MINI GRAMMAR CHALLENGE

If you've already completed Activity 7 in this book, you'll be familiar with 着 **zhe** and how it can be used in the structure *subject + verb + 着* **zhe** *+ object* to describe the state of a person. This time, we're going to use 着 **zhe** in a different construction, which you can use to describe what you see:

location + verb + 着 **zhe** *+ topic*

In this construction, no one is doing anything, so there is no subject. You can use it to describe what you see rather than reporting the action that someone is carrying out or describing a person's current condition. 祝你成功! **Zhù nǐ chénggōng!**

* * *

Let's start by comparing the following sentences:

Tā zhèngzài qiáng shàng guà yí ge sháozi.
她正在墙上挂一个勺子。
She is hanging a ladle on the wall.

Qiáng shàng guà zhe yí ge sháozi.
墙上挂着一个勺子。
A ladle is hanging on the wall.

The first sentence states that someone is doing something, while the second is not an ongoing action but a description of what you see.

When you want to offer a description of what you see, the structure is:

location + a verb + 着 **zhe** + *the topic*

In the example above, 墙上 **qiáng shàng** (*on the wall*) is the location, 挂着 **guà zhe** (*to be hanging*) is the verb and 一个勺子 **yí ge sháozi** (*a ladle*) is the topic.

To practise describing what we see using this structure, let's do the following exercises.

EXERCISE 1

Decide which is the correct translation of each English sentence and circle either A or B.

  1. *There is a map hanging on the wall.*
     A. 墙上挂着一张地图。
     B. 她正在墙上挂地图。

2. *The character for "person" is written on the white paper.*
   A. 一个人正在白纸上写"人"字。
   B. 白纸上写着一个"人"字。

3. *There are eight people sitting around the table.*
   A. 桌子四周坐着八个人。
   B. 八个人正围着桌子坐。

EXERCISE 2

Fill in the blanks by choosing the most appropriate *verb* + 着 zhe
phrase from the following:

写着 xiě zhe, 画着 huà zhe, 坐着 zuò zhe, 摆着 bǎi zhe,
挂着 guà zhe, 站着 zhàn zhe, 躺着 tǎng zhe

1. 墙上的那张油画上 ✎_____一只狗。
   Qiáng shàng de nà zhāng yóuhuà shàng ✎_____
   yì zhī gǒu.

2. 那张A4纸上 ✎_____三个大字"我爱你"。
   Nà zhāng A4 zhǐ shàng ✎_____ **sān ge dà zì**
   "wǒ ài nǐ".

3. 那面墙上 ✎_____一张世界地图。**Nà miàn**
   qiáng shàng ✎_____ **yì zhāng shìjiè dìtú.**

4. 老师正在讲课。教室里 ✎_____20个
   学生。**Lǎoshī zhèngzài jiǎngkè. Jiàoshì lǐ**
   ✎_____ **20 ge xuésheng.**

5. 有人敲门, 我打开门一看, 发现屋子外面
   ✎_____一个小孩子。**Yǒurén qiāomén,**
   wǒ dǎkāi mén yí kàn, fāxiàn wūzi wàimiàn
   ✎_____ **yí ge xiǎoháizi.**

6. 桌子上 ✎_____ 很多饭菜。**Zhuōzi shàng**

   ✎_____ **hěn duō fàncài.**

7. 床上 ✎_____ 一个人在睡觉。**Chuáng**

   shàng ✎_____ **yí ge rén zài shuìjiào.**

* * *

When you're ready, you can check your answers on pages 69-70.

13

五和六
Wǔ hé liù

IDIOMATICALLY SPEAKING

The focus of this activity is a selection of Chinese idioms that contain the numbers 五 **wǔ** and 六 **liù**. Let's look at the following idioms and their word-for-word translations, followed by their idiomatic meanings.

人五人六   **rén wǔ rén liù**
LITERAL TRANSLATION: *person five person six*
IDIOMATIC TRANSLATION: *to be pretentious*

五冬六夏   **wǔ dōng liù xià**
LITERAL TRANSLATION: *five winters six summers*
IDIOMATIC TRANSLATION: *in all seasons*

五颜六色   **wǔ yán liù sè**
LITERAL TRANSLATION: *five colours six hues*
IDIOMATIC TRANSLATION: *colourful*

五雀六燕   **wǔ què liù yàn**
LITERAL TRANSLATION: *five sparrows six swallows*
IDIOMATIC TRANSLATION: *similar in weight*

EXERCISE

Choose one of the idioms to fill in each blank so that the sentences make sense.

1. 这个西瓜跟那个西瓜差不多一样重，不过是
   ✎_____ 的区别。**Zhè ge xīguā gēn nà ge xīguā chàbuduō yíyàng zhòng, bùguò shì ✎_____ de qūbié.**

2. 那个家伙在别人面前总是 ✎_____ 的，好像他很重要似的。**Nà ge jiāhuo zài bié ren miànqián zǒng shì ✎_____ de, hǎoxiàng tā hěn zhòngyào sìde.**

3. 老人是一个认真的门卫，✎_____ 都在看护着我们的小区。**Lǎorén shì yí ge rènzhēn de ménwèi, ✎_____ dōu zài kānhù zhe wǒmen de xiǎoqū.**

4. 春天来了，花园里开着 ✎_____ 的花朵。**Chūntiān lái le, huāyuán lǐ kāi zhe ✎_____ de huāduǒ.**

* * *

太棒了! **Tài bàng le!** When you're ready, you can check your answers on page 71.

14

打麻将

Dǎ májiàng

SAY WHAT YOU SEE

In this activity, we're focusing on writing skills. Take a close look at the image on the next page, then use the suggested phrases on the next page to help you write a short description of the scene. This scene shows a group of people playing 麻将 **májiàng**, known in English as Mahjong. This game originated in China and is popular to this day. It is usually played by four people and involves a set of tiles.

To describe this scene, you may find the following structure useful: *verb + resultative*. This structure is explained in a Mini Grammar Challenge on page 51. 加油! **Jiāyóu!**

SUGGESTED PHRASES

打麻将 **dǎ májiàng**	*to play Mahjong*
游戏 **yóuxì**	*game*
桌子上摆着 **zhuōzishàng bǎi zhe**	*there are … on the table*
麻将牌 **májiàngpái**	*Mahjong tile*
老人 **lǎorén**	*older people*
手 **shǒu**	*hand*
是男的 **shì nán de**	*to be male*
是女的 **shì nǚ de**	*to be female*
不说话 **bù shuōhuà**	*not talking*
坐在那里 **zuòzài nàlǐ**	*to sit there*
穿着 **chuānzhe**	*to be wearing (clothes)*
戴着 **dàizhe**	*to be wearing (accessories)*
花格短袖衬衫 **huāgé duǎnxìu chènshān**	*a checked short-sleeved shirt*
一块手表 **yíkuài shǒubiǎo**	*one watch, a watch*
左边 **zuǒbiān**	*on the left*
花衬衫 **huā chènshān**	*a flowery top*
手镯 **shǒuzhuó**	*a bracelet*

认真地 rènzhēnde   *focused*
背景 bèijǐng   *background*
黑板 hēibǎn   *a blackboard*
歌词 gēcí   *musical lyrics*

_____

_____

_____

_____

_____

_____

_____

* * *

If you'd like to see what we came up with, turn to page 72.

15

一寸光阴一寸金

Yícùn guāngyīn yícùn jīn

GUIDED TRANSLATION

In this Guided Translation, we're going to look at another well-known Chinese saying. By breaking it down word by word, we'll figure out its meaning. 开始吧! **Kāishǐ ba!**

一寸光阴一寸金，
寸金难买寸光阴。

CHINESE PROVERB

一寸光阴一寸金, 寸金难买寸光阴。**Yícùn guāngyīn yícùn jīn, cùnjīn nán mǎi cùn guāngyīn.**

* * *

LANGUAGE EXPLANATION

Let's take a closer look at the language used in this saying.

We'll begin with 一寸 **yícùn**. These two characters mean *one inch*.

The third and fourth characters, 光阴 **guāngyīn**, mean *time*.

You'll recognise the next two characters as we have a repetition of 一寸 **yícùn**. This time, the item being mentioned is 金 **jīn**, *gold*. Obviously, neither time nor gold is measured in inches, but the words of the saying are equating a certain amount of time with a certain amount of money.

The second half of the sentence further develops the meaning of the saying. You'll now be able to work out the first two characters after the comma, 寸金 **cùnjīn**.

Next, 难买 **nán mǎi** means *can't buy*.

Finally, the last three characters, 寸光阴 **cùn guāngyīn**, repeat an earlier part of the saying.

Now, can you put all this together to figure out the meaning of the saying 一寸光阴一寸金, 寸金难买寸光阴 **yícùn guāngyīn yícùn jīn, cùnjīn nán mǎi cùn guāngyīn?**

✎ _____

_____

_____

* * *

When you think you know the meaning, turn to pages 72-73 to find the answer.

16

单立人(亻)和双立人(彳)
Dānlìrén hé shuānglìrén
WORD BUILDER

Our focus for this activity is on how to build your Chinese vocabulary with the help of the "person" radical 亻 and the "double-person" radical 彳. The radical 亻 comes from a character you're very familiar with: 人 **rén** (*person*). When it is used as a radical for the characters that are related to a person, it is placed to the left of the character and is changed to 亻.

* * *

Let's see some characters that have the person radical 亻:

伴 **bàn**		*companion*
信 **xìn**		*letter*
仁 **rén**		*benevolence*
使 **shǐ**		*ambassador*
侍 **shì**		*to attend, to serve (e.g. in a restaurant)*

Now let's look at some characters that have the double-person radical 彳:

行 **háng**	*a line of people*
彼 **bǐ**	*the other*
街 **jiē**	*street*
征 **zhēng**	*to enlist soldiers*
徒 **tú**	*apprentice, to apprentice*

As you can see, characters with the person radical 亻 are often related to a person, while characters with the double-person radical 彳 are often related to multiple people.

As you'll see in the next examples, however, not all characters that contain the radical 亻 or 彳 have such an immediately obvious connection to a person or to multiple people. The next characters we'll look at come in pairs – notice how the meaning changes entirely depending on whether the radical is 亻 or 彳.

仿 **fǎng**	*to imitate*	彷 **páng**	*to hesitate*
住 **zhù**	*to live*	往 **wǎng**	*towards*
侍 **shì**	*to attend*	待 **dài**	*to wait until*
佯 **yáng**	*to fake*	徉 **yáng**	*to walk around*
彼 **bǐ**	*evil*	彼 **bǐ**	*the other, that*
倘 **tǎng**	*if*	徜 **cháng**	*to walk around*
佛 **fó**	*Buddha*	彿 **fú**	*as if*

49

EXERCISE

Now let's practise the difference between these pairs. Use the pinyin and the English translation to help you decide whether 亻 or 彳 should be added to the left of the following characters. Then, write the whole character in the box. Try your best without referring to the list above.

e.g. 史　[使]　　**shǐ**　　*ambassador*

1. 主　　　　**zhù**　　*to live*

2. 寺　　　　**dài**　　*to wait until*

3. 羊　　　　**yáng**　　*to fake*

4. 弗　　　　**fó**　　*Buddha*

5. 方　　　　**páng**　　*to hesitate*

＊ ＊ ＊

你真棒! **Nǐ zhēn bàng!** Find the answers on page 73.

17

看和看见
Kàn hé kànjiàn
MINI GRAMMAR CHALLENGE

In this activity, we're going to practise using verbs with resultative complements to demonstrate the result of an action. 祝你成功! **Zhù nǐ chénggōng!**

* * *

Let's look at the following dialogue:

A: **Qǐng kàn nà ge zì.**
请看那个字。 *Please look at that character.*

B: **Wǒ kànjiàn nà ge zì le.**
我看见那个字了。 *I saw that character.*

As you can see, sentence A with 看 **kàn** + *object* (the character) only refers to the effort, while sentence B with 看见 **kànjiàn** + *object* refers to the result. Every time we add a resultative complement after the verb, we are indicating that the action has led to a result. Note that sentences with a positive resultative complement usually have 了 **le** at the end to indicate the result or change. Let's look at some more examples:

Wǒ kànwán le.
我看完了。   *I read it and finished reading it.*

Wǒ chībǎo le.
我吃饱了。   *I ate and I'm full now.*

Wǒ tīngdǒng le.
我听懂了。   *I listened and understood.*

Of course, these are just some examples, and the complements can also be used after many other verbs.

If you made the effort but without result, then you add 没有 **méi yǒu** before the verb:

Wǒ méi yǒu kànwán.
我没有看完。   *I haven't finished reading it.*

Wǒ méi yǒu chībǎo.
我没有吃饱。   *I am not full yet.*

Wǒ méi yǒu tīngdǒng.
我没有听懂。   *I haven't understood it yet.*

If you believe you won't achieve the desired result, you can add 不 **bù** between the verb and the resultative complement and say:

Wǒ kàn bù wán.
我看不完。   *I can't finish reading it.*

Wǒ chī bù bǎo.

我吃不饱。 *I can't have enough food.*

Wǒ tīng bù dǒng.

我听不懂。 *I can't understand it.*

Let's think about the context in which you may use the examples with 没有 **méi yǒu** and those with 不 **bù**. Imagine someone is speaking to you in Mandarin but you are struggling to understand what they're saying, so they offer to switch to Cantonese. If you don't speak Cantonese, you could reply by saying: 我听不懂广东话 **wǒ tīng bù dǒng guǎngdōnghuà**. This is because you don't have the ability to understand Cantonese since you haven't learned the language. Instead, if you want to ask them to repeat what they said in Mandarin so that you can try again to understand it, you could say: 我没有听懂 **wǒ méi yǒu tīngdǒng**. This is because you have the ability to understand what they said and, although you made the effort the first time you heard it, you didn't understand.

Now, let's do some exercises to practise using the construction *verb + resultative complement*.

EXERCISE 1

Decide which is the correct translation of each English sentence and circle either A or B.

1. *I read and understood this book.*
    A. 我看懂这本书了。
    B. 我看这本书了。

2. *He said that someone was knocking on the door, but I didn't hear it.*
   A. 他说有人敲门，可是我没有听到。
   B. 他说有人敲门，可是我听不到。

3. *I saw a person walking there.*
   A. 我看见一个人在走路。
   B. 我看一个人在走路。

EXERCISE 2

Fill in blanks by choosing the most appropriate *verb + resultative complement* phrase from the following:

没有做完 méi yǒu zuòwán, 吃饱 chībǎo,
看不完 kàn bù wán

1. 我 ✎_____ 了，不想再吃了。
   Wǒ ✎_____ le, bù xiǎng zài chī le.

2. 你还 ✎_____ 你的功课，不可
   以出去玩。 Nǐ hái ✎_____ nǐ de
   gōngkè, bù kěyǐ chūqù wán.

3. 这本书太长了，我三天 ✎_____ 。
   Zhè běn shū tài cháng le, wǒ sān tiān

   ✎_____.

* * *

Once you're happy with your answers, you can check them on pages 73-74.

18

七和八
Qī hé bā
IDIOMATICALLY SPEAKING

Our focus for this activity is a collection of Chinese idioms that contain the numbers 七 qī and 八 bā. Let's look at the following idioms, see their word-for-word translations and find out their idiomatic meanings.

七上八下   qī shàng bā xià
LITERAL TRANSLATION: *seven ups eight downs*
IDIOMATIC TRANSLATION: *nervous, agitated*

七嘴八舌   qī zuǐ bā shé
LITERAL TRANSLATION: *seven mouths eight tongues*
IDIOMATIC TRANSLATION: *many people speaking at the same time*

七手八脚   qī shǒu bā jiǎo
LITERAL TRANSLATION: *seven hands eight feet*
IDIOMATIC TRANSLATION: *many people trying to help*

七扭八歪   qī niǔ bā wāi
LITERAL TRANSLATION: *seven twists eight slants*
IDIOMATIC TRANSLATION: *twisted and slanted, misshapen*

七折八扣   **qī zhé bā kòu**

LITERAL TRANSLATION: *seven discounts eight deductions*

IDIOMATIC TRANSLATION: *large price deductions*

EXERCISE

Choose one of the idioms above to fill in each blank according to the context of the sentence.

1. 开会时大家 ✎_____,都在说话,
   听不清谁在说什么。**Kāihuì shí dàjiā**
   ✎_____ , **dōu zài shuōhuà, tīng**
   bùqīng shéi zài shuō shénme.

2. 这些汉字写得 ✎_____ 的, 很不
   好看。**Zhèxiē hànzì xiě de** ✎_____
   de, hěn bù hǎokàn.

3. 我写的文章交上去了, 还不知道能不能发表, 心里
   ✎_____ 的。**Wǒ xiě de wénzhāng**
   jiāo shàngqù le, hái bù zhīdào néng bù néng fābiǎo, xīnli
   ✎_____ **de.**

4. 他在办公室摔倒了。大家 ✎_____
   把他送到了医院。**Tā zài bàngōngshì shuāidǎo le. Dàjiā**
   ✎_____ **bǎ tā sòngdào le yīyuàn.**

5. 汽车终于卖掉了。✎_____
   以后, 没有剩下多少钱。**Qìchē zhōngyú màidiào le.**
   ✎_____ **yǐhòu, méi yǒu shèngxià**
   duōshǎo qián.

* * *

太棒了! **Tài bàng le!** When you're ready, you can check the answers on pages 74-75.

19

在咖啡馆
Zài kāfēiguǎn

SAY WHAT YOU SEE

Have a look at this picture of a scene in a café. How would you describe it? Use the suggested phrases on the next page to help you write three to five sentences about what you can see. 加油! **Jiāyóu!**

SUGGESTED PHRASES

一男二女 yì nán èr nǚ	*one man and two women*
咖啡 kāfēi	*coffee*
咖啡馆 kāfēiguǎn	*café*
喝 hē	*to drink*
聊天 liáotiān	*to chat*
中间的人 zhōngjiān de rén	*the person in the middle*
左边的人 zuǒbiān de rén	*the person on the left*
右边的人 yòubiān de rén	*the person on the right*
穿 chuān	*to put on, to wear (clothes)*
穿着* chuān zhe	*to be wearing (clothes)*
条纹 tiáowén	*striped*
上衣 shàngyī	*top, clothes for the upper body*
浅色 qiǎnsè	*light-coloured*
戴着 dài zhe	*to be wearing (accessories)*
一副眼镜 yí fù yǎnjìng	*a pair of glasses*
一顶帽子 yì dǐng màozi	*a hat*
桌子上有 zhuōzi shàng yǒu	*on the table there is / are*
杯子 bēizi	*cup*
一束花 yí shù huā	*a bunch of flowers*
看起来 kànqǐlái	*it looks like, it appears*
高兴 gāoxìng	*happy*

*We suggest you use the structure *verb* + 着 zhe to describe someone wearing an item of clothing or an accessory. If this structure using 着 zhe is new to you, you can find a Mini Grammar Challenge on this topic on page 22.

Now it's over to you to write your description. Write in Chinese characters, pinyin or a mixture of the two – whatever is most useful for you and most appropriate for your level.

_____

_____

_____

_____

_____

_____

_____

_____

_____

_____

_____

_____

_____

_____

_____

_____

* * *

When you're ready, turn to page 75 to see a suggested answer.

20

十有八九

Shí yǒu bā jiǔ

GUIDED TRANSLATION

If you have already completed the Idiomatically Speaking activities in this book, you'll know some Chinese idioms that use the numbers one to eight. In this Guided Translation, let's add one final number idiom to your collection and learn one that contains the numbers eight, nine and ten. Here it is: 十有八九 **shí yǒu bā jiǔ**.

* * *

LANGUAGE EXPLANATION

Let's take a closer look at the language used in this idiom.

The language in this expression is very straightforward. You'll recognise three numbers: 十 **shí** (*ten*), 八 **bā** (*eight*) and 九 **jiǔ** (*nine*).

The remaining word in the saying is 有 **yǒu**, meaning *has*.

Putting the four words together, our literal translation would be something like *ten has eight or nine.*

If we think about this further, when ten has already got eight or nine, it means it is almost at 100 per cent.

So, have you worked out the meaning of this idiom? Put your understanding to the test by translating the following sentences from Chinese into English.

1. 那些人中文说得非常好，十有八九是中国人。
   Nàxiē rén Zhōngwén shuō de fēicháng hǎo, shí yǒu bā jiǔ shì Zhōngguórén.

   ✎ _____

   _____

2. 我三天找不到我的手机了，十有八九是丢了。
   Wǒ sān tiān zhǎobudào wǒ de shǒujī le, shí yǒu bā jiǔ shì diū le.

   ✎ _____

   _____

3. 他最近不找我出去饭馆吃饭了，十有八九是又有女朋友了。 **Tā zuìjìn bù zhǎo wǒ chūqù fànguǎn chīfàn le, shí yǒu bā jiǔ shì yòu yǒu nǚpéngyou le.**

   ✎ _____

   _____

4. 这里的人十有八九都没有去过中国。 **Zhèlǐ de rén shí yǒu bā jiǔ dōu méi yǒu qù guò Zhōngguó.**

   ✎ _____

   _____

* * *

When you're ready, turn to page 76 to read the meaning of the idiom, as well as the translations of the sentences.

5-MINUTE COFFEE BREAKS

I. 城市生活 Chéngshì shēnghuó
WORD BUILDER

1. 我不舒服。请带我去医院。Wǒ bù shūfu. Qǐng dài wǒ qù yīyuàn.

   TRANSLATION: *I don't feel well. Please take me to hospital.*

2. 我要坐地铁。请问，**地铁站**怎么走？Wǒ yào zuò dìtiě. Qǐngwèn, **dìtiě zhàn** zěnme zǒu?

   TRANSLATION: *I need to take the subway. How do I get to the subway station, please?*

3. 我要买水。哪里有**商店**？Wǒ yào mǎi shuǐ. Nǎlǐ yǒu **shāngdiàn**?

   TRANSLATION: *I need to buy some water. Where is there a shop/store?*

4. 我要坐车，附近有**汽车站**吗？Wǒ yào zuòchē, fùjìn yǒu **qìchēzhàn** ma?

    TRANSLATION: *I need to take a bus. Is there a bus stop nearby?*

5. 我还没有看见过大熊猫，我们今天去**动物园**吧。
    Wǒ hái méi yǒu kànjiàn guo dàxióngmāo, wǒmen jīntiān qù **dòngwùyuán** ba.

    TRANSLATION: *I haven't seen a giant panda yet. Let's go to the zoo today.*

2. 怎么用"了" Zěnme yòng "le"
MINI GRAMMAR CHALLENGE

1. 他喝茶了。**Tā hē chá le.**

    TRANSLATION: *He has drunk tea.*

2. 她哥哥写毛笔字了。**Tā gēge xiě máobǐzì le.**

    TRANSLATION: *Her (older) brother has written characters with a brush.*

3. 我妈妈今天做鱼了。**Wǒ māma jīntiān zuò yú le.**

    TRANSLATION: *My mum has cooked fish today.*

4. 姐姐在家洗衣服了。**Jiějie zàijiā xǐ yīfu le.**

    TRANSLATION: *My (older) sister has done her laundry at home.*

5. 妹妹今天游泳了。**Mèimei jīntiān yóuyǒng le.**

    TRANSLATION: *My (younger) sister has swum today.*

4. 年夜饭 Niányèfàn
SAY WHAT YOU SEE

HERE'S WHAT WE CAME UP WITH:

Yì jiā rén zhèng zài chú fáng chī nián yè fàn. Zhuō zi
一 家 人 正 在 厨 房 吃 年 夜 饭。 桌 子

zhōu wéi zuò zhe wǔ ge rén. Xiǎo nǚ hái zuǒ biān zuò
周 围 坐 着 五 个 人。 小 女 孩 左 边 坐

zhe tā de mā ma, mā ma zuǒ biān zuò zhe yé ye,
着 她 的 妈 妈, 妈 妈 左 边 坐 着 爷 爷,

yé ye zuǒ biān zuò zhe bà ba, bà ba zuǒ biān zuò
爷 爷 左 边 坐 着 爸 爸, 爸 爸 左 边 坐

zhe nǎi nai. Měi ge rén miàn qián bǎi zhe wǎn, pán zi
着 奶 奶。 每 个 人 面 前 摆 着 碗、 盘 子

hé kuài zi. Zhuō zi zhōng jiān bǎi zhe hěn duō hǎo chī
和 筷 子。 桌 子 中 间 摆 着 很 多 好 吃

de fàn cài, qí zhōng yǒu huǒ guō, yú, ròu, mó gu, gè
的 饭 菜, 其 中 有 火 锅、 鱼、 肉、 蘑 菇、 各

zhǒng qīng cài. Qiáng shàng guà zhe sháo zi, chǎn zi hé liǎng
种 青 菜。 墙 上 挂 着 勺 子、 铲 子 和 两

ge xiǎo hóng dēng lóng. Yì jiā rén zài pèng bēi, shuō xīn
个 小 红 灯 笼。 一 家 人 在 碰 杯, 说 新

nián kuài lè. Tā men dōu hěn gāo xìng.
年 快 乐。 他 们 都 很 高 兴。

5. 三人行，必有我师 Sān rén xíng, bì yǒu wǒ shī
GUIDED TRANSLATION

TRANSLATION: *When three are walking together, I am sure to find a teacher among them.*

Confucius teaches us to be modest and to always learn from others. This quotation suggests that we can learn from anyone and that there is always something to be learned from a person.

6. 三点水和两点水 Sāndiǎnshuǐ hé liǎngdiǎnshuǐ
WORD BUILDER

1. 冷 lěng
2. 泪 lèi
3. 凉 liáng
4. 汁 zhī
5. 凝 níng
6. 洗 xǐ
7. 凄 qī
8. 河 hé

7. 怎么用"着"1 Zěnme yòng "zhe" 1
MINI GRAMMAR CHALLENGE

EXERCISE 1:

1. B. 进来的人都穿着黑色的衣服。 **Jìnlái de rén dōu chuān zhe hēisè de yīfu.**

2. B. 那个人走了。他穿着条纹上衣。 **Nà ge rén zǒu le. Tā chuān zhe tiáowén shàngyī.**

3. A. 中间那个人穿着红色的大衣。 **Zhōngjiān nà ge rén chuān zhe hóngsè de dàyī.**

EXERCISE 2:

I. A.　左边那个人戴着一副大眼镜。**Zuǒbiān nà ge rén dài zhe yí fù dà yǎnjìng.**

2. B.　出门之前请戴帽子。**Chūmén zhīqián qǐng dài màozi.**

3. A.　照片里的小女孩头上戴着一朵花。**Zhàopiàn lǐ de xiǎo nǚhái tóushàng dài zhe yì duǒ huā.**

9. 在公园 Zài gōngyuán
SAY WHAT YOU SEE

HERE'S WHAT WE CAME UP WITH:

Zhè	shì	zài	yí	ge	gōng	yuán	lǐ.	Gōng	yuán	lǐ	rén	hěn
这	是	在	一	个	公	园	里。	公	园	里	人	很

duō.	Tiān	qì	hěn	nuǎn	huo,	hěn	duō	rén	dōu	chuān	duǎn	yī
多。	天	气	很	暖	和,	很	多	人	都	穿	短	衣

duǎn	kù.	Yǒu	de	rén	zhèng	zài	yì	tiáo	xiǎo	lù	shàng	pǎo
短	裤。	有	的	人	正	在	一	条	小	路	上	跑

bù,	yǒu	de	rén	zhèng	zài	zǒu	bù,	yǒu	de	rén	zhèng	zài
步,	有	的	人	正	在	走	步,	有	的	人	正	在

qí	zì	xíng	chē,	hái	yǒu	de	rén	zài	zhào	kàn	hái	zi.
骑	自	行	车,	还	有	的	人	在	照	看	孩	子。

Zuǒ	biān	de	yì	nán	yì	nǚ	yì	biān	pǎo	bù,	yì	biān
左	边	的	一	男	一	女	一	边	跑	步,	一	边

liáo	tiān.	Tā	men	zhèng	zài	xiàng	wǒ	men	pǎo	lái.	Zhōng	jiān
聊	天。	他	们	正	在	向	我	们	跑	来。	中	间

de	nán	rén	zài	qí	zì	xíng	chē.	Yòu	biān	de	nǚ	rén
的	男	人	在	骑	自	行	车。	右	边	的	女	人

méi	yǒu	pǎo	bù.	Tā	zhèng	zài	zhào	kàn	yīng	ér	chē	lǐ
没	有	跑	步。	她	正	在	照	看	婴	儿	车	里

de	hái	zi.	Tā	hěn	kě	néng	shì	xiǎo	hái	zi	de	mā
的	孩	子。	她	很	可	能	是	小	孩	子	的	妈

ma.	Yí	ge	xiǎo	gū	niáng	zài	bāng	zhù	nǚ	rén	zhào	kàn
妈。	一	个	小	姑	娘	在	帮	助	女	人	照	看

chē	lǐ	de	hái	zi.	Tā	hěn	kě	néng	shì	xiǎo	hái	zi
车	里	的	孩	子。	她	很	可	能	是	小	孩	子

de	jiě	jie.	Gōng	yuán	lǐ	xiǎo	lù	liǎng	páng	yǒu	hěn	duō
的	姐	姐。	公	园	里	小	路	两	旁	有	很	多

shù,	hái	yǒu	lù	dēng.
树,	还	有	路	灯。

10. 太阳从西边出来 Tàiyáng cóng xībiān chūlái
GUIDED TRANSLATION

TRANSLATION: *The sun rises in the west* (literally *the sun comes out from the west*).

But how can the sun rise in the west? You're right, the sun rises in the east! This is why this saying is used to mean that something will never happen.

Let's look at two examples to see how the idiom 太阳从西边出来 **tàiyáng cóng xībiān chūlái** is used in context:

Rúguǒ xiǎng děng nà ge lǎobǎn gěi gōngrén zhǎng gōngzī, nà yào děng tàiyáng cóng xībiān chūlái.

如果想等那个老板给工人涨工资，那要等太阳从西边出来。

If you want to wait for that boss to raise the workers' salaries, you need to wait until the sun rises in the west.

Tā cónglái hěn xiǎoqì, kěshì jīntiān yào qǐng dàjiā chīfàn。Tàiyáng cóng xībiān chūlái le ma?

他从来很小气，可是今天要请大家吃饭。太阳从西边出来了吗？

He's always very stingy, but today he wants to treat everyone to dinner. Did the sun rise in the west?

12. 怎么用"着"2 Zěnme yòng "zhe" 2
MINI GRAMMAR CHALLENGE

EXERCISE 1:

1. A. 墙上挂着一张地图。 **Qiáng shàng guà zhe yì zhāng dìtú.**

2. B. 白纸上写着一个"人"字。 **Bái zhǐ shàng xiě zhe yí ge "rén" zì.**

3. A. 桌子四周坐着八个人。 **Zhuōzi sìzhōu zuò zhe bā ge rén.**

EXERCISE 2:

1. 墙上的那张油画上画着一只狗。 Qiáng shàng de nà zhāng yóuhuà shàng **huà zhe** yì zhī gǒu.

   TRANSLATION: *That painting on the wall shows a dog.*

2. 那张A4纸上写着三个大字"我爱你"。 Nà zhāng A4 zhǐ shàng **xiě zhe** sān ge dà zì "wǒ ài nǐ".

   TRANSLATION: *On that A4 sheet, three large words are written: "I love you".*

3. 那面墙上挂着一张世界地图。 Nà miàn qiáng shàng **guà zhe** yì zhāng shìjiè dìtú.

   TRANSLATION: *There's a map of the world hanging on that wall.*

4. 老师正在讲课。教室里坐着20个学生。 Lǎoshī zhèngzài jiǎngkè. Jiàoshì lǐ **zuò zhe** 20 ge xuésheng.

   TRANSLATION: *The teacher is giving a lesson. 20 students are sitting in the classroom.*

5. 有人敲门，我打开门一看，发现屋子外面站着一个小孩子。 Yǒurén qiāomén, wǒ dǎkāi mén yí kàn, fāxiàn wūzi wàimiàn **zhàn zhe** yí ge xiǎoháizi.

   TRANSLATION: *Someone knocked at the door. I opened the door and saw a small child standing outside the house.*

6. 桌子上摆着很多饭菜。 Zhuōzi shàng **bǎi zhe** hěn duō fàncài.

   TRANSLATION: *There are many dishes on the table.*

7. 床上躺着一个人在睡觉。 Chuáng shàng **tǎng zhe** yí ge rén zài shuìjiào.

   TRANSLATION: *There's a person lying on the bed asleep.*

13. 五和六 Wǔ hé liù
IDIOMATICALLY SPEAKING

1. 这个西瓜跟那个西瓜差不多一样重, 不过是**五雀六燕**的区别。 Zhè ge xīguā gēn nà ge xīguā chàbuduō yíyàng zhòng, bùguò shì **wǔ què liù yàn** de qūbié.

   TRANSLATION: *This watermelon and that watermelon are almost as heavy as each other. There isn't much difference in weight.*

2. 那个家伙在别人面前总是**人五人六**的, 好像他很重要似的。 Nà ge jiāhuo zài biéren miànqián zǒngshì **rén wǔ rén liù** de, hǎoxiàng tā hěn zhòngyào sìde.

   TRANSLATION: *That guy is always pretentious in front of others, as if he is a very important person.*

3. 老人是一个认真的门卫, **五冬六夏**都在看护着我们的小区。 Lǎorén shì yí ge rènzhēn de ménwèi, **wǔ dōng liù xià** dōu zài kānhù zhe wǒmen de xiǎoqū.

   TRANSLATION: *The old man is a dutiful security guard. He protects our neighbourhood all year round.*

4. 春天来了, 花园里开着**五颜六色**的花朵。 Chūntiān lái le, huāyuán lǐ kāi zhe **wǔ yán liù sè** de huāduǒ.

   TRANSLATION: *Spring is here and the garden is full of colourful flowers.*

14. 打麻将 Dǎ májiàng
SAY WHAT YOU SEE

HERE'S WHAT WE CAME UP WITH:

Zhè zhāng zhào piān li, sì ge lǎo rén zuò zài nà li
这 张 照 片 里, 四 个 老 人 坐 在 那 里

dǎ má jiàng. Zhuō zi shàng bǎi zhe hěn duō má jiàng pái.
打 麻 将。 桌 子 上 摆 着 很 多 麻 将 牌。

Sì ge rén li sān ge shì nǚ de, yí ge shì nán
四 个 人 里 三 个 是 女 的 一 个 是 男

de. Nà ge nán de chuān zhe yí jiàn duǎn xiù huā gé
的。 那 个 男 的 穿 着 一 件 短 袖 花 格

chèn shān, dài zhe yí kuài shǒu biǎo. Zhào piān zuǒ biān de
衬 衫, 戴 着 一 块 手 表。 照 片 左 边 的

nǚ de chuān zhe huā chèn shān, tā de zuǒ yòu shǒu dōu
女 的 穿 着 花 衬 衫, 她 的 左 右 手 都

dài zhe yí ge shǒu zhuó. Tā men zài rèn zhēn de dǎ
戴 着 一 个 手 镯。 他 们 在 认 真 地 打

má jiàng. Bèi jǐng hēi bǎn shang xiě zhe hàn zì hé gē
麻 将。 背 景 黑 板 上 写 着 汉 字 和 歌

cí.
词。

15. 一寸光阴一寸金 Yícùn guāngyīn yícùn jīn
GUIDED TRANSLATION

TRANSLATION: *One inch of time is one inch of gold, but even if you have one inch of gold, you can't buy one inch of time.*

This saying is similar to the English saying *time is money, but money can't buy time.*

16. 单立人(亻)和双立人(彳) Dānlìrén hé shuānglìrén
WORD BUILDER

1. 住 zhù
2. 待 dài
3. 佯 yáng
4. 佛 fó
5. 彷 páng

17. 看和看见 Kàn hé kànjiàn
MINI GRAMMAR CHALLENGE

EXERCISE 1:

1. A. 我看懂这本书了。 Wǒ kàndǒng zhè běn shū le.

2. A. 他说有人敲门，可是我没有听到。 Tā shuō yǒu rén qiāomén, kěshì wǒ méi yǒu tīngdào.

3. A. 我看见一个人在走路。 Wǒ kànjiàn yí ge rén zài zǒulù.

EXERCISE 2:

1. 我吃饱了，不想再吃了。 Wǒ **chībǎo** le, bùxiǎng zài chī le.
   TRANSLATION: *I ate enough, I don't want to eat any more.*

2. 你还没有做完你的功课，不可以出去玩。 Nǐ hái **méi yǒu zuòwán** nǐ de gōngkè, bù kěyǐ chūqù wán.
   TRANSLATION: *You haven't finished your homework, so you can't go out to play.*

3. 这本书太长了，我三天**看不完**。 Zhè běn shū tài cháng le, wǒ sān tiān **kàn bù wán**.

TRANSLATION: *This book is too long. I can't finish it within three days.*

18. 七和八 Qī hé bā
IDIOMATICALLY SPEAKING

1. 开会时大家**七嘴八舌**，都在说话，听不清谁在说什么。 Kāihuì shí dàjiā **qī zuǐ bā shé**, dōu zài shuōhuà, tīng bù qīng shéi zài shuō shénme.

TRANSLATION: *During the meeting, everyone was talking at the same time. No one could hear who was saying what.*

2. 这些汉字写得**七扭八歪**的，很不好看。 Zhèxiē hànzì xiě de **qī niǔ bā wāi** de, hěn bù hǎokàn.

TRANSLATION: *These Chinese characters were scribbled sloppily and they look ugly.*

3. 我写的文章交上去了，还不知道能不能发表，心里**七上八下**的。 Wǒ xiě de wénzhāng jiāo shàngqù le, hái bù zhīdào néng bù néng fābiǎo, xīnli **qī shàng bā xià** de.

TRANSLATION: *I submitted the article I wrote, but I don't know if it will be able to be published. I feel very nervous.*

4. 他在办公室摔倒了。大家**七手八脚**把他送到了医院。 Tā zài bàngōngshì shuāidǎo le. Dàjiā **qī shǒu bā jiǎo** bǎ tā sòngdào le yīyuàn.

TRANSLATION: *He fell in the office. Everyone hurried to get him to the hospital.*

5. 汽车终于卖掉了。**七折八扣**以后，没有剩下多少钱。

Qìchē zhōngyú màidiào le. **Qī zhé bā kòu** yǐhòu, méi yǒu shèngxià duōshǎo qián.

TRANSLATION: *The car was finally sold. After all kinds of deductions, not much money was left.*

19. 在咖啡馆 Zài kāfēiguǎn
SAY WHAT YOU SEE

HERE'S WHAT WE CAME UP WITH:

Yì	nán	èr	nǚ	sān	ge	péng	you	zài	yì	jiā	kā	fēi
一	男	二	女	三	个	朋	友	在	一	家	咖	啡

guǎn	hē	kā	fēi	liáo	tiān.	Zhōng	jiān	de	rén	chuān	zhe	tiáo
馆	喝	咖	啡	聊	天。	中	间	的	人	穿	着	条

wén	shàng	yī.	Tā	zuǒ	biān	de	rén	chuān	zhe	qiǎn	sè	shàng
纹	上	衣。	她	左	边	的	人	穿	着	浅	色	上

yī,	hái	dài	zhe	yí	fù	dà	yǎn	jìng.	Tā	yòu	biān	de
衣,	还	戴	着	一	副	大	眼	镜。	她	右	边	的

rén	dài	zhe	yì	dǐng	mào	zi.	Zhuō	zi	shàng	yǒu	yì	xiē
人	戴	着	一	顶	帽	子。	桌	子	上	有	一	些

bēi	zi	hé	yí	shù	huā.	Tā	men	kàn	qǐ	lái	hěn	gāo
杯	子	和	一	束	花。	他	们	看	起	来	很	高

xìng,	dōu	zài	xiào.
兴,	都	在	笑。

20. 十有八九 Shí yǒu bā jiǔ
GUIDED TRANSLATION

The idiom 十有八九 **shí yǒu bā jiǔ** means that something is almost certain or very likely, or that something is true in the majority of cases.

Here are the translations:

1. *Those people speak very good Chinese. They are most likely Chinese.*
2. *I haven't seen my mobile phone for three days. I've probably lost it.*
3. *He hasn't asked me to go out to eat at a restaurant lately. Chances are that he has got a girlfriend again.*
4. *Most of the people here have never been to China.*

10-MINUTE COFFEE BREAKS

CHECKLIST

10-MINUTE COFFEE BREAKS

Number Focus
- ❑ 重要年份 Zhòngyào niánfèn - page 92
- ❑ 现在几点？Xiànzài jǐdiǎn? - page 110
- ❑ 金婚和银婚 Jīnhūn hé yínhūn - page 131
- ❑ 成千上万 Chéng qiān shàng wàn - page 151

Taste Bud Tantaliser
- ❑ 番茄鸡蛋 Fānqié jīdàn - page 95
- ❑ 包饺子 Bāo jiǎozi - page 114
- ❑ 饿了吗？È le ma? - page 135
- ❑ 面条 Miàntiáo - page 155

21

翻译挑战 1

Fānyì tiǎozhàn 1

TRANSLATION CHALLENGE

In this Translation Challenge, we'd like you to translate some sentences from English into Chinese. These sentences will help you practise using 了 le, as well as your translation skills in general. If you need help, you can find some hints at the end of this section. Answers will be provided in both characters and pinyin, so have a go at writing as many of the characters as you can, but write in pinyin for any that you don't know. 祝你成功! **Zhù nǐ chénggōng!**

* * *

1. I've cleaned my room today.

🖉_____

_____

_____

2. She has bought three movie tickets.

   _____

   _____

3. My younger brother has read many books.

   _____

   _____

   _____

4. Her mother has cooked food for us.

   _____

   _____

   _____

5. She has already done her laundry.

   _____

   _____

   _____

HINTS

If you need some help, you may find the following hints useful.

1. For the first sentence, put 了 **le** at the end of the sentence to indicate that you have completed the task of cleaning your room.

2. In the second sentence, 了 **le** should be placed before the quantity rather than at the end of the sentence.

3. In the third sentence, the rule for sentence two still applies, even though the quantity is not an exact amount. 了 **le** is therefore going to come in front of *many*.

4. In the fourth sentence, remember to put 了 **le** at the end of the sentence. Also remember to place *for us* before the verb.

5. In the fifth sentence, 了 **le** should go at the end of the sentence again.

* * *

真好! **Zhēn hǎo!** Once you're happy with your translations, turn to pages 161-162 to find our suggested answers.

22

孔子
Kǒngzǐ

FAMOUS CHINESE SPEAKERS

In this activity, we'll be working on reading comprehension. The following text is about a very famous Chinese speaker, Confucius. Use the vocabulary list and the pinyin (if you need it) to help you as you read through the text, then answer the comprehension questions to test your understanding.

* * *

Kǒng	zǐ	shì	Zhōng	guó	gǔ	dài	sī	xiǎng	jiā,	zhèng	zhì	jiā,
孔	子	是	中	国	古	代	思	想	家、	政	治	家、

jiào	yù	jiā.	Tā	shēng	zài	gōng	yuán	qián	551	nián,	sǐ	zài
教	育	家。	他	生	在	公	元	前	551	年,	死	在

gōng	yuán	qián	479	nián.	Tā	yì	shēng	jiāo	le	hěn	duō	hěn
公	元	前	479	年。	他	一	生	教	了	很	多	很

duō	xué	sheng,	yí	gòng	yǒu	sān	qiān	duō	rén,	qí	zhōng	qī
多	学	生,	一	共	有	三	千	多	人,	其	中	七

shí èr ge xué sheng hòu lái fēi cháng yǒu míng. Tā shuō
十 二 个 学 生 后 来 非 常 有 名。 他 说

guò, wú lùn shì shéi, měi ge rén dōu kě yǐ shòu jiào
过, 无 论 是 谁, 每 个 人 都 可 以 受 教

yù. Tā duì dài dà jiā dōu hěn hǎo, zūn zhòng měi yí
育。 他 对 待 大 家 都 很 好, 尊 重 每 一

ge rén. Tā hái shuō guò, "jǐ suǒ bú yù, wù shī yú
个 人。 他 还 说 过, "己 所 不 欲, 勿 施 于

rén". Yì si shì, rú guǒ nǐ zì jǐ bù xiǎng yào bié
人"。 意 思 是, 如 果 你 自 己 不 想 要 别

rén nà yàng duì dài nǐ, nǐ yě bú yào nà yàng duì
人 那 样 对 待 你, 你 也 不 要 那 样 对

dài bié rén. Nǐ tóng yì Kǒng zǐ de zhè xiē huà ma?
待 别 人。 你 同 意 孔 子 的 这 些 话 吗?

VOCABULARY

古代	gǔdài	*ancient times*
思想家	sīxiǎngjiā	*thinker*
政治家	zhèngzhìjiā	*statesman*
教育家	jiàoyùjiā	*educator*
公元前	gōngyuánqián	*before Common Era*
对待	duìdài	*to treat, to deal with*
尊重	zūnzhòng	*to respect*

己所不欲，勿施于人。
Jǐ suǒ bú yù, wù shī yú rén.

Don't do to others what you don't want others to do to you.

COMPREHENSION QUESTIONS

Answer the following questions in English.

1. What sort of person is Confucius described as in the first sentence?

   ✎_____

   _____

2. When was he born and when did he die?

   ✎_____

   _____

3. How many students did he teach in his life? How many of them became famous?

   ✎_____

   _____

4. What did he believe about education?

   ✎_____

   _____

5. What does the sentence 己所不欲，勿施于人 mean? Try to answer without referring to the vocabulary list.

✎ _____

_____

* * *

Once you're happy with your answers, check with the answers section on page 162.

23

独体和集体量词
Dútǐ hé jítǐ liàngcí
FOR GOOD MEASURE

As you'll already know from your learning experience, in Chinese we use both numbers and measure words (also known as "counters" or "classifiers") to count things. In this activity, we'll focus on some of these 量词 **liàngcí** (*measure words*), specifically individual and collective measure words. Read the short explanation below, then have a go at the exercises that follow. 加油! **Jiāyóu!**

* * *

Measure words can be divided into individual measure words and collective measure words. Let's look at the six phrases below:

A. 一张地图 **yì zhāng dìtú**   *one map*
B. 两条河 **liǎng tiáo hé**   *two rivers*
C. 五个人 **wǔ ge rén**   *five people*
D. 三双筷子 **sān shuāng kuàizi**   *three pairs of chopsticks*
E. 一群学生 **yì qún xuésheng**   *a group of students*
F. 两打鸡蛋 **liǎng dá jīdàn**   *two dozen eggs*

As you can see, the measure words in phrases A, B and C are individual measure words.

张 **zhāng** in phrase A serves as a measure word for something flat, for example pieces of paper, tickets, tables and photos.

条 **tiáo** in phrase B serves as a measure word for something long, for example scarves, ties, fish and snakes.

个 **ge** in phrase C serves as a measure word for a person, as well as many other things. 个 **ge** is the most commonly used measure word. If ever you are unsure which measure word to use, use 个 **ge**.

The measure words in phrases D, E and F are collective measure words.

双 **shuāng** in phrase D is a measure word for something in pairs, for example pairs of shoes, socks, gloves and earrings.

群 **qún** in phrase E is a measure word for something in groups, for example groups of sheep, lions, horses, fish and people.

打 **dá** (not to be confused with **dǎ**, which has the same character but instead means *to beat*) in phrase F is a measure word for something in dozens, for example dozens of eggs, beers, cookies and flowers.

Now, let's practise using individual and collective measure words in the following exercises.

EXERCISE 1 - MATCH

Draw a line to match each phrase with its translation.

一条鱼	*three pairs of shoes*
两个妹妹	*a fish*
三双鞋子	*a group of workers*
一群工人	*two friends*
三条领带	*a dozen eggs*
十张桌子	*five pieces of red paper*
两个朋友	*two younger sisters*
四双筷子	*four pairs of chopsticks*
五张红纸	*ten tables*
一打鸡蛋	*three ties*

EXERCISE 2 - FILL IN THE GAPS

Complete the following sentences by adding in the correct measure words.

1. 爸爸今天买了三 ✎_____ 围巾。 **Bàba jīntiān mǎi le sān ✎_____ wéijīn.**

2. 我们是六 ✎_____ 人，为什么只给我们五 ✎_____ 筷子？ **Wǒmen shì liù ✎_____ rén, wèishénme zhǐ gěi wǒmen wǔ ✎_____ kuàizi?**

3. 她有两 ✎_____ 电影票。 **Tā yǒu liǎng ✎_____ diànyǐngpiào.**

4. 妹妹今天穿了一 ✎_____ 白裙子，很漂亮。 **Mèimei jīntiān chuān le yì ✎_____ bái qúnzi, hěn piàoliang.**

5. 一 ✎_____ 玫瑰花多少钱？Yì ✎_____ méiguīhuā
   duōshǎo qián?

6. 他家有一大 ✎_____ 山羊。Tā jiā yǒu yí dà ✎_____
   shānyáng.

7. 我有很多 ✎_____ 鞋。你挑一 ✎_____ 吧。
   Wǒ yǒu hěn duō ✎_____ xié. Nǐ tiāo yì ✎_____ ba.

8. 一 ✎_____ 白纸也很好。你想画什么，就画什么。
   Yì ✎_____ bái zhǐ yě hěn hǎo. Nǐ xiǎng huà shénme, jiù
   huà shénme.

9. 你的房间里有几 ✎_____ 床？Nǐ de fángjiān lǐ yǒu jǐ
   ✎_____ chuáng?

10. 今天商店的鸡蛋很便宜，妈妈买了两 ✎_____ 。
    够我们吃十天了。Jīntiān shāngdiàn de jīdàn hěn piányi,
    māma mǎi le liǎng ✎_____. Gòu wǒmen chī shí tiān le.

*   *   *

太棒了！Tài bàng le! When you're ready, you can check your
answers on pages 163-164.

24

重要年份
Zhòngyào niánfèn
NUMBER FOCUS

Like in any language, numbers are very important in Chinese. In this activity, we're going to practise them in the context of dates. And we couldn't possibly talk about dates in Chinese without learning about some of the important dynasties of China over the past 3,000 years. But before we practise those historical dates, let's do a quick review of the basic numbers in Chinese.

* * *

一 yī	one
二 èr	two
三 sān	three
四 sì	four
五 wǔ	five
六 liù	six
七 qī	seven

八	**bā**	*eight*
九	**jiǔ**	*nine*
十	**shí**	*ten*
零	**líng**	*zero*

Below you will find a list of important years when dynasties were founded (or ended) in China. First, write the years as numerical figures. Then, have a go at writing each year next to its corresponding event. It may help you to know that 公元 **gōngyuán** refers to Common Era (CE), while 公元前 **gōngyuánqián** refers to Before Common Era (BCE). 祝你成功! **Zhù nǐ chénggōng!**

DATES

Write the following years in numerical figures.

1. 公元前二二一年 ✎_____
2. 公元前二零六年 ✎_____
3. 公元二二零年 ✎_____
4. 公元六一八年 ✎_____
5. 公元一二零六年 ✎_____
6. 公元一三六八年 ✎_____
7. 公元一九一一年 ✎_____
8. 公元一九四九年 ✎_____

IMPORTANT EVENTS

Fill in the gap in each sentence based on the hints in English, using the dates from the list above. Write in Chinese characters.

1. 秦国在公元前✎_____ 年统一
   了中国。
   The State of Qin unified the whole country in 221 BCE.

2. 汉朝在公元前✎_____年建立。
   The Han Dynasty was established in 206 BCE.

3. 汉朝在公元✎_____ 年结束。
   The Han Dynasty ended in 220 CE.

4. 唐朝在公元✎_____ 年建立。
   The Tang Dynasty was established in 618 CE.

5. 元朝在公元✎_____ 年建立。
   The Yuan Dynasty was established in 1206.

6. 明朝在公元✎_____ 年建立。
   The Ming Dynasty was established in 1368.

7. 中华民国在✎_____ 年建立。
   The Republic of China was established in 1911.

8. 中华人民共和国在✎_____
   年建立。
   The People's Republic of China was established in 1949.

* * *

Once you've had a go, turn to pages 164-165 to check your answers.

25

番茄鸡蛋
Fānqié jīdàn
TASTE BUD TANTALISER

In our Taste Bud Tantalisers, we use a recipe as a reading text and work through an exercise based on the language used in it. 番茄鸡蛋 **fānqié jīdàn** (*tomato and egg stir fry*) is a classic Chinese dish that is easy to find in most restaurants in China or in Chinatowns around the world. It's a dish that's easy to make at home and is very tasty! Read the recipe for 番茄鸡蛋 **fānqié jīdàn**, then have a go at the exercises that follow. If you'd like an extra challenge, try reading the text and completing the exercises before looking at the vocabulary list. 祝你成功! **Zhù nǐ chénggōng!**

* * *

Cái	liào
材	料

fān	qié	liǎng	ge
番	茄	两	个

jī	dàn	sān	ge
鸡	蛋	三	个

盐 适 量
yán shì liàng

酱 油 适 量
jiàng yóu shì liàng

葱 花 适 量
cōng huā shì liàng

做 法
Zuò fǎ

(一) 番 茄 洗 干 净, 切 块。
Fān qié xǐ gān jìng, qiē kuài.

(二) 鸡 蛋 打 散, 加 入 适 量 盐。
Jī dàn dǎ sǎn, jiā rù shì liàng yán.

(三) 锅 里 热 油, 炒 蛋, 盛 出。
Guō lǐ rè yóu, chǎo dàn, chéng chū.

(四) 锅 里 热 油, 炒 番 茄 块。
Guō lǐ rè yóu, chǎo fān qié kuài.

(五) 加 入 鸡 蛋、 盐 和 酱 油。
Jiā rù jī dàn, yán hé jiàng yóu.

(六) 加 入 葱 花, 就 可 以 盛 出
Jiā rù cōng huā, jiù kě yǐ chéng chū

吃 了。
chī le.

VOCABULARY

材料 **cáiliào**   *ingredients*

盐 **yán**   *salt*

适量 **shìliàng**   *a little, according to taste*

酱油 **jiàngyóu**	*soy sauce*
葱花 **cōnghuā**	*chopped spring onions / green onions*
干净 **gānjìng**	*clean*
切块 **qiēkuài**	*to cut into cubes*
打散 **dǎsǎn**	*to stir/beat, to break up*
加入 **jiārù**	*to add*
锅 **guō**	*pot*
炒 **chǎo**	*to stir-fry*
盛出 **chéngchū**	*to serve, to take out from the pan/pot*

EXERCISE - TRUE OR FALSE?

Are the following statements true or false, 对还是不对 **duì háishì bú duì**? Circle your answer for each statement and if false, give the correct statement.

1. You need three tomatoes and two eggs.

   对 | 不对

   ✎ _____

   _____

2. 葱花 is a kind of flower.

   对 | 不对

   ✎ _____

   _____

3. The tomatoes should be cut into cubes.

   对 ｜ 不对

   ✎_____

   _____

4. The tomatoes should be stir-fried first and the eggs should be stir-fried second.

   对 ｜ 不对

   ✎_____

   _____

5. The chopped green onions should be added last before serving.

   对 ｜ 不对

   ✎_____

   _____

* * *

太棒了！ **Tài bàng le!** When you're ready, turn to page 166 to find the answers.

26

翻译挑战 2
Fānyì tiǎozhàn 2
TRANSLATION CHALLENGE

In this Translation Challenge, you're going to be translating some sentences from English into Chinese, this time focusing on using modal verbs in particular. Answers will be provided both in characters and pinyin, so write your answers in whichever way is appropriate for your level. If you need some help, you can find a hint for each sentence at the end of this section.

* * *

1. May I sit here?

✎ _____

_____

_____

2. Students should hand in their papers before class.

✎_____

_____

_____

3. Do you think he will come today?

✎_____

_____

_____

4. She wants to go swimming, not shopping.

✎_____

_____

_____

5. We have to clean the room after breakfast.

✎_____

_____

_____

HINTS

If you need some help, you may find the following hints useful.

1. In the first sentence, use 可以 **kěyǐ** or 能 **néng** before the verb to ask for permission.

2. In the second sentence, use 应该 **yīnggāi** or 得 **děi** before the verb to express obligation.

3. In the third sentence, use 会 **huì** or 能 **néng** before the verb because you're predicting whether or not something will happen.

4. In the fourth sentence, use 想 **xiǎng** or 要 **yào** before the verb to indicate intention.

5. In the fifth sentence, use 必须 **bìxū** or 得 **děi** before the verb to indicate obligation.

* * *

Once you're happy with your translations, turn to pages 166-168 to read our suggested answers and explanations.

27

三毛

Sān Máo

FAMOUS CHINESE SPEAKERS

In this reading comprehension activity, we're going to learn about the Taiwanese writer 三毛 **Sān Máo**. We recommend noting down any vocabulary that is new to you to help you remember it, before testing your understanding with the comprehension questions. If you'd like an extra challenge, try ignoring the pinyin and the vocabulary list at first. Remember, they're always there if you need help afterwards.

* * *

Sān	Máo	shì	Tái	wān	yǒu	míng	de	zuò	jiā.	Sān	Máo
三	毛	是	台	湾	有	名	的	作	家。	三	毛

shēng	yú	1943	nián,	sǐ	yú	1991	nián.	Sān	Máo	shì	tā
生	于	1943	年,	死	于	1991	年。	三	毛	是	她

de	bǐ	míng,	tā	de	míng	zi	shì	Chén	Píng.	Tā	fā
的	笔	名,	她	的	名	字	是	陈	平。	她	发

表的书有:《撒哈拉的故事》、《雨季不再来》、《送你一匹马》、《谈心》、《我的宝贝》、《亲爱的三毛》等等。三毛的丈夫荷西是一个西班牙人,但是早在1979年就死了。三毛在非洲生活过,也在美洲生活过。三毛的书大多都非常浪漫,里面有感人的爱情故事,有非洲、美洲的风土人情,有大沙漠,也有大森林。这些都是一般的读者看不到的,因此他们都非常喜欢看三毛的书。虽然三毛的书非常受欢迎,但是她却开玩笑说自己的书不太好,只值三毛钱,所以笔名是"三毛"。

103

VOCABULARY

台湾	**Táiwān**	*Taiwan*
作家	**zuòjiā**	*writer*
生于	**shēngyú**	*to be born in (the year of)*
死于	**sǐyú**	*to die in (the year of)*
笔名	**bǐmíng**	*pen name*
发表	**fābiǎo**	*to publish*
撒哈拉	**Sāhālā**	*Sahara Desert*
雨季	**yǔjì**	*rainy season*
谈心	**tán xīn**	*heart-to-heart (talk)*
宝贝	**bǎo bèi**	*baby*
等等	**děngděng**	*and so on*
荷西	**Héxī**	*Jose*
西班牙	**Xībānyá**	*Spain*
非洲	**Fēizhōu**	*Africa*
美洲	**Měizhōu**	*the Americas*
浪漫	**làngmàn**	*romantic*
感人的	**gǎnrén de**	*touching, moving*
爱情故事	**àiqíng gùshì**	*love story*
风土人情	**fēng tǔ rén qíng**	*traditions of the local people*
沙漠	**shāmò**	*desert*
森林	**sēnlín**	*forest*
一般的	**yìbān de**	*ordinary*
值	**zhí**	*worth*
三毛钱	**sān máo qián**	*three dimes**

*Of course, this doesn't translate literally as *three dimes* but just as a dime is a tenth of one dollar, in Chinese currency a 毛 **máo** is a tenth of one 元 **yuán**.

COMPREHENSION QUESTIONS

Answer the following questions in English.

1. In which year was San Mao born and in which year did she die?

   _____

   _____

2. Of all the books mentioned, which book's title has something to do with Africa? And which book title mentions her name?

   _____

   _____

3. Did San Mao ever live in Africa?

   _____

   _____

4. Why do so many people like San Mao's works?

   _____

   _____

5. Why did San Mao give herself the pen name "San Mao"?

   _____

   _____

* * *

太棒了！**Tài bàng le!** Once you're happy with your answers, turn to page 168 to check them.

28

临时量词
Línshí liàngcí
FOR GOOD MEASURE

In this activity, we are looking at 临时量词 **línshí liàngcí** – temporary measure words. Temporary measure words are nouns that are temporarily used as measure words. Read the explanation below, then have a go at the exercises that follow to put into practice what you've learned. 加油！**Jiāyóu!**

* * *

In Chinese, we have a saying:

> **Yàoxiǎng gěi xuésheng yì bēi shuǐ, lǎoshī zuìshǎo xūyào yǒu yì tǒng shuǐ.**
> 要想给学生一杯水，老师最少需要有一桶水。
> *If a teacher wants to give students one cup of water, they should have at least one bucket of water ready.*

As you can see, the nouns 杯 **bēi** (*cup*) and 桶 **tǒng** (*bucket*) are temporarily serving as measure words.

Let's look at some other nouns that can be used as temporary measure words:

一船新汽车 yì chuán xīn qì chē	*a shipload of new cars*
两卡车土 liǎng kǎchē tǔ	*two truckloads of dirt*
三碗汤 sān wǎn tāng	*three bowls of soup*
四袋土豆 sì dài tǔdòu	*four bags of potatoes*
五瓶水 wǔ píng shuǐ	*five bottles of water*
两勺油 liǎng sháo yóu	*two spoonfuls of oil*
一桌报纸 yì zhuō bàozhǐ	*a table of newspapers*
一屋人 yì wū rén	*a house (full) of people*
十箱书 shí xiāng shū	*ten boxes of books*
三篮苹果 sān lán píngguǒ	*three baskets of apples*

As you can see, nouns can serve as temporary measure words, as long as they are some kind of container.

Also note that 的 **de** can be added between a temporary measure word and the noun, for example: 一屋(的)人 yì **wū (de) rén**, 十箱(的)书 shí **xiāng (de) shū**.

Let's practise using temporary measure words in the following two exercises.

EXERCISE 1 - MATCH

Draw a line to match each phrase with its translation.

三篮桃子	*a shipload of new cars*
一屋烟	*two truckloads of rocks*
两勺醋	*three bowls of soup*
四袋红薯	*four bags of sweet potatoes*
两卡车石头	*five bottles of wine*
一船新汽车	*two spoonfuls of vinegar*
三碗汤	*a table (full) of letters*
五瓶酒	*a house (full) of smoke*
一桌信	*ten boxes of clothes*
十箱衣服	*three baskets of peaches*

EXERCISE 2 - FILL IN THE GAPS

Complete the following sentences by adding in the correct temporary measure words, using the hints in English to help you.

1. 爸爸今天买了一 ✎_____ 酱油。**Bàba jīntiān mǎi le yì** ✎_____ **jiàngyóu.** *(one bottle of soy sauce)*

2. 我们是六个人, 为什么只给我们五 ✎_____ 汤? **Wǒmen shì liù ge rén, wèishénme zhǐ gěi wǒmen wǔ** ✎_____ **tāng?** *(five bowls of soup)*

3. 屋子里有三 ✎_____ 书。 **Wūzi lǐ yǒu sān** ✎_____ **shū.** *(three boxes of books)*

4. 你不是想看报纸吗? 这里有一 ✎_____ 报纸。 **Nǐ bú shì xiǎng kàn bàozhǐ ma? Zhèlǐ yǒu yì** ✎_____ **bàozhǐ.** *(a table of newspapers)*

5. 两 ✎_____ 土一共要多少钱? **Liǎng** ✎_____ **tǔ yígòng yào duōshǎo qián?** *(two truckloads of dirt)*

6. 学生给老师送去了三 ✎_____ 苹果。 **Xuésheng gěi lǎoshī sòngqù le sān** ✎_____ **píngguǒ.** *(three baskets of apples)*

7. 我只要用两 ✎_____ 油。 **Wǒ zhǐyào yòng liǎng** ✎_____ **yóu.** *(two spoonfuls of oil)*

8. 学校这个冬天要买四 ✎_____ 土豆。 **Xuéxiào zhège dōngtiān yào mǎi sì** ✎_____ **tǔdòu.** *(four bags of potatoes)*

9. 我们会有更多的新汽车。明天会来一✎_____
   新汽车。 **Wǒmen huì yǒu gèng duō de xīn qìchē.**
   Míngtiān huì lái yì ✎_____ xīn qìchē. *(a shipload of new cars)*

10. 家里有一✎_____ 人在等你。你快回来吧。 **Jiālǐ**
    yǒu yì ✎_____ rén zài děng nǐ. Nǐ kuài huílái ba.
    (a house full of people)

* * *

太棒了！**Tài bàng le!** The answers can be found on pages 169-170.

29

现在几点?
Xiànzài jǐdiǎn?
NUMBER FOCUS

What time is it? To answer this question, we have to learn to use numbers in Chinese in the context of time. We'll start by looking at some examples as a reminder of how to specify hours, minutes and the time of day when giving the time in Chinese.

* * *

一点 yì diǎn		1:00
两点 liǎng diǎn		2:00
三点 sān diǎn		3:00

Note that 一点 yì diǎn could refer to either 1 AM or 1 PM. The same goes for any time where the speaker hasn't specified the time of day.

十四点 shí sì diǎn 14:00

二十二点 èr shí èr diǎn 22:00

一点五分 yì diǎn wǔ fēn 1:05

两点一刻 liǎng diǎn yí kè 2:15, *quarter past 2*

三点半 sān diǎn bàn 3:30

差一刻五点 chà yí kè wǔ diǎn 4:45, *quarter to 5*

凌晨五点 língchéng wǔ diǎn 5:00 AM

上午九点 shàngwǔ jiǔ diǎn 9:00 AM

下午三点 xiàwǔ sān diǎn 3:00 PM

晚上十点 wǎnshàng shí diǎn 10:00 PM

夜里十一点 yèli shí yī diǎn 11:00 PM

半夜十二点 bànyè shí èr diǎn 12:00 AM, *midnight*

零点 líng diǎn 00:00

EXERCISE 1 - WRITE IN DIGITS

Now it's over to you to work out the following times. Here's the first one as an example:

上午九点十分 = 9:10 AM

1. 上午九点

✎_____

2. 晚上八点五分

✎_____

3. 差一刻四点

✎_____

4. 十一点

 ✎ _____

5. 四点半

 ✎ _____

6. 凌晨四点

 ✎ _____

7. 二十二点

 ✎ _____

8. 下午两点

 ✎ _____

EXERCISE 2 - WRITE IN CHINESE

Now translate the following times into Chinese. Write in Chinese characters or in pinyin – whichever is most appropriate for your level.

I. 3:00 PM

 ✎ _____

2. 2:30 PM

 ✎ _____

3. 9:45 AM

 ✎ _____

4. 2:15 AM

 ✎ _____

5. II:OO AM

✎ _____

6. 9:30 PM

✎ _____

7. 8:OO AM

✎ _____

8. 5:45 PM

✎ _____

* * *

Once you've completed both exercises, turn to page 171 to check your answers.

30

包饺子
Bāo jiǎozi
TASTE BUD TANTALISER

饺子 **jiǎozi** (*dumplings*) are one of the most famous foods from China. 饺子 **jiǎozi** are especially popular in the north of the country during festivals such as the New Year. Family members and friends make and eat dumplings together, so they are part of an important Chinese tradition. While it will take you longer than 10 minutes to make 饺子 **jiǎozi**, you can study and understand the recipe in that time. So, let's learn how to make dumplings.

* * *

Cái	liào
材	料

bái	cài	yì	kē		
白	菜	一	颗		
zhū	ròu	xiàn	yí	bàng
猪	肉	馅	一	磅

cōng sān kē
葱 三 颗

jiāng fěn liǎng sháo
姜 粉 两 勺

yán sì sháo
盐 四 勺

shí yóu liǎng sháo
食 油 两 勺

jiàng yóu liǎng sháo
酱 油 两 勺

jiǎo zi pí liǎng bāo
饺 子 皮 两 包

Zuò fǎ
做 法

(一) Bǎ zhū ròu xiàn fàng zài yí ge pén
把 猪 肉 馅 放 在 一 个 盆
lǐ, fàng jìn shǎo liàng de shí yóu, yán,
里, 放 进 少 量 的 食 油、盐、
jiàng yóu, jiāng fěn bàn yún.
酱 油、姜 粉 拌 匀。

(二) Bǎ bái cài xǐ gān jìng duò suì. Duò
把 白 菜 洗 干 净 剁 碎。剁
qián shàng miàn sǎ liǎng sháo yán, duò hòu
前 上 面 撒 两 勺 盐, 剁 后
bǎ shuǐ jǐ chū lái.
把 水 挤 出 来。

(三)
Bǎ jǐ gān shuǐ de bái cài xiàn fàng
把 挤 干 水 的 白 菜 馅 放
dào pén lǐ hé ròu xiàn bàn yún, chéng
到 盆 里 和 肉 馅 拌 匀，成
wéi jiǎo zi xiàn.
为 饺 子 馅。

(四)
Bǎ yì zhāng jiǎo zi pí píng fàng zài
把 一 张 饺 子 皮 平 放 在
yì zhī shǒu shàng, lìng yì zhī shǒu zhān
一 只 手 上，另 一 只 手 沾
shuǐ, bǎ jiǎo zi pí de wài quān zhān
水，把 饺 子 皮 的 外 圈 沾
shī. Rán hòu jiǎo zi pí zhōng jiān fàng
湿。然 后 饺 子 皮 中 间 放
jìn yì xiē jiǎo zi xiàn.
进 一 些 饺 子 馅。

(五)
Zuì hòu bàn hé jiǎo zi pí, bǎ liǎng
最 后 半 合 饺 子 皮，把 两
biān de jiǎo zi pí niē jǐn zài yì
边 的 饺 子 皮 捏 紧 在 一
qǐ, niē chéng zhě zi gèng hǎo, zhè yàng
起，捏 成 褶 子 更 好，这 样
yí ge jiǎo zi jiù bāo hǎo le.
一 个 饺 子 就 包 好 了。

(六)
Zài yí ge dà guō lǐ shāo shuǐ. Děng
在 一 个 大 锅 里 烧 水。等
shuǐ kāi le yǐ hòu, bǎ sān shí ge
水 开 了 以 后，把 三 十 个

饺 子 一 起 放 进 去。煮 十
jiǎo zi yì qǐ fàng jìn qù. Zhǔ shí

分 钟 以 后，捞 出 来 就 可
fēn zhōng yǐ hòu, lāo chū lái jiù kě

以 吃 了。
yǐ chī le.

VOCABULARY

包饺子 **bāo jiǎozi**		*to make dumplings*
一磅猪肉馅 **yí bàng zhūròu xiàn**		*one pound of ground pork*
姜粉 **jiāngfěn**		*ginger powder*
一勺盐 **yì sháo yán**		*a spoonful of salt*
一棵白菜 **yì kē báicài**		*one napa (a type of cabbage)*
盆 **pén**		*bowl, basin*
拌匀 **bànyún**		*to stir until evenly mixed*
剁碎 **duòsuì**		*to chop into small pieces*
撒盐 **sǎyán**		*to sprinkle salt*
挤干 **jǐgān**		*to squeeze out water until dry*
沾湿 **zhānshī**		*to wet*
外圈 **wàiquān**		*outer circle*
半合 **bànhé**		*half fold, to fold one half over the other*
捏紧 **niējǐn**		*to squeeze tight*
褶子 **zhězi**		*wrinkles*
锅 **guō**		*pot*

烧水 shāoshuǐ   *to boil water*
煮 zhǔ   *to cook with water*
捞出 lāochū   *to take out from the pot*

COMPREHENSION QUESTIONS

Answer the following questions in English.

1. How much ground pork do you need?

   ✎_____

2. How much ginger powder do you need?

   ✎_____

3. What ingredients do you add when you stir the ground pork in a bowl?

   ✎_____

4. How many wrappers do you use for each dumpling?

   ✎_____

5. True or false? You put the raw dumplings into the water before it's boiling.

   ✎_____

6. For how long do you boil the dumplings before you take them
   out to eat?

   _____

* * *

Once you're happy with your answers, turn to page 172 to check
them.

31

翻译挑战 3
Fānyì tiǎozhàn 3
TRANSLATION CHALLENGE

In this Translation Challenge, we are going to translate some questions into Chinese, using either characters or pinyin. Have a go on your own first, but if you need some help you can turn to the end of this section to find a hint for each sentence. We'll start with a straightforward one, then we'll move onto some other question forms.

* * *

I. Does she speak Arabic?

✎_____

_____

_____

2. He doesn't have any friends here, right?

    ✎ _____

    _____

    _____

3. Are you French?

    ✎ _____

    _____

    _____

4. Have you got a torch / flashlight?

    ✎ _____

    _____

    _____

5. Would you like to drink coffee or tea?

    ✎ _____

    _____

    _____

6. Will you or your girlfriend go to the USA?

    ✎ _____

    _____

    _____

HINTS

If you need some help, you may find the following hints useful.

1. In sentence 1, use 吗 **ma** at the end of the statement to ask a straightforward question.

2. In sentence 2, use 对吗 **duì ma** to form a question in which you're asking for confirmation.

3. Try using 是不是 **shìbúshì** in sentence 3, so that your question literally reads *are you or aren't you*.

4. This time, in sentence 4, use 有没有 **yǒu méi yǒu** so that you are literally asking *have you or haven't you*.

5. In sentence 5, use 还是 **háishì** to suggest alternatives.

6. We can also use 还是 **háishì** in sentence 6.

* * *

Once you're happy with your translations, turn to pages 172-173 to find our suggested answers.

32

庄子
Zhuāngzǐ
FAMOUS CHINESE SPEAKERS

In this activity, we're going to learn about another famous Chinese speaker by reading a dialogue between two famous ancient philosophers. The text describes an anecdote about 庄子 **Zhuāngzǐ** and 惠子 **Huìzǐ**, two Chinese philosophers from the 4th century BCE. Read the text, with the help of the vocabulary list, then answer the comprehension questions that follow to test what you've understood. 加油! **Jiāyóu!**

* * *

Zhuāng	zǐ	shì	Zhōng	guó	yí	wèi	yǒu	míng	de	zhé	xué	jiā.
庄	子	是	中	国	一	位	有	名	的	哲	学	家。

Yì	tiān	tā	hé	péng	yǒu	Huì	zǐ	zài	hé	biān	sàn	bù.
一	天	他	和	朋	友	惠	子	在	河	边	散	步。

Tā	men	kàn	dào	yì	qún	yú	zài	hé	lǐ	zì	yóu	de
他	们	看	到	一	群	鱼	在	河	里	自	由	地

yóu lái yóu qù, jiù yǒu le xià miàn de duì huà:
游 来 游 去， 就 有 了 下 面 的 对 话：

Zhuāng zǐ: Nǐ kàn, hé lǐ de yú duō me kuài lè!
庄 子： 你 看， 河 里 的 鱼 多 么 快 乐！

Huì zǐ: Nǐ bú shì yú, nǐ zěn me zhī dào yú
惠 子： 你 不 是 鱼， 你 怎 么 知 道 鱼

hěn kuài lè?
很 快 乐？

Zhuāng zǐ: Nǐ bú shì wǒ, zěn me zhī dào wǒ bù
庄 子： 你 不 是 我， 怎 么 知 道 我 不

zhī dào yú hěn kuài lè?
知 道 鱼 很 快 乐？

Huì zǐ: Nǐ bú shì wǒ, zěn me zhī dào wǒ bù
惠 子： 你 不 是 我， 怎 么 知 道 我 不

zhī dào nǐ bù zhī dào yú kuài lè bú
知 道 你 不 知 道 鱼 快 乐 不

kuài lè?
快 乐？

Tā men de duì huà hái huì zhè yàng jì xù xià qù,
他 们 的 对 话 还 会 这 样 继 续 下 去，

dàn shì nǐ jué de shéi gèng yǒu dào lǐ?
但 是 你 觉 得 谁 更 有 道 理？

VOCABULARY

哲学家	zhéxuéjiā	*philosopher*
散步	sànbù	*to take a walk*
一群鱼	yì qún yú	*a school of fish*
自由地	zìyóu de	*freely*
游来游去	yóu lái yóu qù	*to swim to and fro, to swim around*
下面的	xiàmiàn de	*the following*
对话	duìhuà	*dialogue*
多么	duōme	*so*
继续下去	jìxù xiàqù	*to continue, to go on*
有道理	yǒudàolǐ	*reasonable*

COMPREHENSION QUESTIONS

Answer the questions in English.

1. Where were Zhuangzi and Huizi taking a walk?

_____

_____

2. What did they see in the river?

_____

_____

3. What were the fish doing?

✎_____

_____

4. What did Zhuangzi say about the fish?

✎_____

_____

5. What did Huizi say about what Zhuangzi said?

✎_____

_____

6. How did Zhuangzi argue back?

✎_____

_____

* * *

真棒! **Zhēn bàng!** When you're ready, you can check your answers on page 174.

33

动作量词
Dòngzuò liàngcí
FOR GOOD MEASURE

Our focus for this activity is 动作量词 **dòngzuò liàngcí** – verbal measure words. Read the explanation below, then have a go at the exercises that follow to put your understanding to the test. 加油! **Jiāyóu!**

* * *

There are two types of verbal measure words in Chinese. The first type is individual verbal measure words. These measure words are used for the number of occurrences and the duration of actions. The most common individual verbal measure words are 次 **cì**, 遍 **biàn**, 下 **xià** and 场 **chǎng**.

Let's look at some examples with individual verbal measure words:

去两次 **qù liǎng cì**	*to go twice*
看三遍 **kàn sān biàn**	*to read three times*

Both 次 **cì** and 遍 **biàn** refer to times of doing something, but 遍 **biàn** places emphasis on the whole process from the beginning to the end, such as reading a book or watching a film.

Now let's look at the individual verbal measure words 下 **xià** and 场 **chǎng**. When you use a verb and 一下 **yí xià** it means you do this action very briefly and quickly. When you use a verb and 一场 **yì chǎng**, it means you do this action for the whole duration of an episode (usually, a sports game or a performance). For example:

问一下	**wèn yí xià**	*to ask quickly*
打两场	**dǎ liǎng chǎng**	*to play two games*
听一场歌剧	**tīng yì chǎng gējù**	*to listen to an opera / one opera*

Now let's look at the second type of verbal measure words. This is where the names of parts of the body or tools are temporarily used as measure words to count the frequency of actions. Let's look at some examples:

亲一口	**qīn yì kǒu**	*to give a quick kiss*
看一眼	**kàn yì yǎn**	*to take a quick look*
切一刀	**qiē yì dāo**	*to make a cut with a knife*
打三锤	**dǎ sān chuí**	*to hammer three times*

Note that 看一眼 **kàn yì yǎn** is a set phrase and we don't change the number before 眼 **yǎn**. Now, let's practise!

EXERCISE 1 - MATCH

Draw a line to match each Chinese phrase with its English translation.

闻一下	*to sniff briefly*
打两场	*to listen briefly*
踢一脚	*to play two games*
切一刀	*to write ten times*
去两次	*to read three times*
砍三斧	*to go twice*
咬一口	*to take a bite*
看三遍	*to kick once*
听一下	*to make a cut with a knife*
写十遍	*to cut three times with an axe*

EXERCISE 2 - FILL IN THE GAPS

Complete the following sentences by adding in the correct measure words, using the hints in English to help you.

1. 爸爸今天看了 ✎＿＿＿＿＿＿ 篮球赛。 **Bàba jīntiān kàn le** ✎＿＿＿＿＿＿ **lánqiú sài.** *(two basketball games)*

2. 老师要我们看这本书，而且还要看 ✎＿＿＿＿＿＿ 。 **Lǎoshī yào wǒmen kàn zhè běn shū, érqiě hái yào kàn** ✎＿＿＿＿＿＿ . *(three times)*

3. 说再见的时候妈妈在她女儿的小脸上亲了 ✎＿＿＿＿＿＿ 。 **Shuō zàijiàn de shíhou māma zài tā nǚ'ér de xiǎo liǎn shàng qīn le** ✎＿＿＿＿＿＿ . *(kissed briefly)*

4. 哥哥经常去中国，已经去了 ✎_____ 。
   Gēge jīngcháng qù Zhōngguó, yǐjīng qù le ✎_____ .
   (went five times)

5. 我们不知道怎么走了。你去问 ✎_____ 。
   Wǒmen bù zhīdào zěnme zǒu le. Nǐ qù wèn ✎_____ .
   (ask briefly)

6. 她只看了 ✎_____ ，就知道那不是她的书包。
   Tā zhǐ kàn le ✎_____ , **jiù zhīdào nà bú shì tā de shūbāo.** *(took a brief look)*

7. 要想知道肉里面做好了没有，切 ✎_____ 一看就知道了。 **Yào xiǎng zhīdào ròu lǐmiàn zuò hǎo le méi yǒu, qiē** ✎_____ **yí kàn jiù zhīdào le.** *(make one cut with a knife)*

8. 要想记住汉字怎么写，每个字要写 ✎_____ 。
   Yào xiǎng jìzhù hànzì zěnme xiě, měi ge zì yào xiě
   ✎_____ . *(write ten times)*

9. 她要和朋友一起去听 ✎_____ 音乐会。 **Tā yào hé péngyou yìqǐ qù tīng** ✎_____ **yīnyuèhuì.** *(one concert)*

* * *

太棒了! **Tài bàng le!** Once you're happy with your answers, turn to pages 174-176 to check them.

34

金婚和银婚
Jīnhūn hé yínhūn
NUMBER FOCUS

The idea of marking wedding anniversaries with special names according to the number of years is a tradition in many cultures across the world. This practice is also popular nowadays in China, as a result of western influence. In this Number Focus activity, let's use this concept to help us practise numbers in Chinese.

* * *

In the following list, you'll find out what each wedding anniversary is traditionally known as. Familiarise yourself with the Chinese characters that are new to you in the list, then have a go at the exercise that follows. Note that 婚 **hūn** is the word for *wedding* or *marriage*. So, for example, 银婚 **yín hūn** translates as *silver wedding anniversary*.

1.	一年 yì nián	纸婚 zhǐ hūn	paper
2.	两年 liǎng nián	棉婚 mián hūn	cotton
3.	三年 sān nián	皮婚 pí hūn	leather
4.	四年 sì nián	花果婚 huāguǒ hūn	flowers and fruit
5.	五年 wǔ nián	木婚 mù hūn	wood
6.	六年 lìu nián	糖婚 táng hūn	sugar
7.	七年 qī nián	黄铜婚 huángtóng hūn	copper
8.	八年 bā nián	青铜婚 qīngtóng hūn	bronze
9.	九年 jiǔ nián	陶婚 táo hūn	pottery
10.	十年 shí nián	锡婚 xī hūn	tin
11.	十一年 shíyī nián	钢婚 gāng hūn	steel
12.	十二年 shíèr nián	丝婚 sī hūn	silk
13.	十三年 shísān nián	花边婚 huābiān hūn	lace
14.	十四年 shísì nián	象牙婚 xiàngyá hūn	ivory
15.	十五年 shíwǔ nián	水晶婚 shuǐjīng hūn	crystal
20.	二十年 èrshí nián	瓷婚 cí hūn	china
25.	二十五年 èrshíwǔ nián	银婚 yín hūn	silver
30.	三十年 sānshí nián	珍珠婚 zhēnzhū hūn	pearl
35.	三十五年 sānshíwǔ nián	珊瑚婚 shānhú hūn	coral
40.	四十年 sìshí nián	红宝石婚 hóngbǎoshí hūn	ruby
45.	四十五年 sìshíwǔ nián	蓝宝石婚 lánbǎoshí hūn	sapphire
50.	五十年 wǔshí nián	金婚 jīn hūn	gold
55.	五十五年 wǔshíwǔ nián	绿宝石婚 lǜbǎoshí hūn	emerald
60.	六十年 lìushí nián	钻石婚 zuànshí hūn	diamond
70.	七十年 qīshí nián	白金婚 báijīn hūn	platinum

EXERCISE

Now try answering the following questions. Answer in full sentences, writing in Chinese characters or pinyin.

1. 结婚五十年是什么婚？ **Jiéhūn wǔshí nián shì shénme hūn?**

   ✎ _____

   _____

2. 结婚十三年是什么婚？ **Jiéhūn shísān nián shì shénme hūn?**

   ✎ _____

   _____

3. 结婚三十年是什么婚？ **Jiéhūn sānshí nián shì shénme hūn?**

   ✎ _____

   _____

4. 结婚四年是什么婚？ **Jiéhūn sì nián shì shénme hūn?**

   ✎ _____

   _____

5. 结婚一年是什么婚？ **Jiéhūn yì nián shì shénme hūn?**

   ✎ _____

   _____

6. 结婚六十年是什么婚？ **Jiéhūn liùshí nián shì shénme hūn?**

✎_____

_____

7. 结婚二十年是什么婚？ **Jiéhūn èrshí nián shì shénme hūn?**

✎_____

_____

8. 你结婚了吗？现在是什么婚？ **Nǐ jiéhūn le ma? Xiànzài shì shénme hūn?**

✎_____

_____

* * *

太棒了！**Tài bàng le!** Once you've finished, turn to page 176 to find the answers.

35

饿了吗？
È le ma?

TASTE BUD TANTALISER

民以食为天 **mín yǐ shí wéi tiān**. This saying translates as *people take food as heaven* and it demonstrates how important food is in Chinese culture. There are therefore many characters in Chinese that share the radical 饣, which is the food radical. In this Taste Bud Tantaliser our text is a dialogue between two friends, which is all about food. Read the dialogue and answer the comprehension questions that follow to test your understanding. As you're reading, look out for the 饣 radical, which appears many times throughout the text.

* * *

Zhāng	Lì:	Nǐ	xiàn	zài	yǒu	jī	è	gǎn	le	ma?
张	丽:	你	现	在	有	饥	饿	感	了	吗？

	Gāng	cái	nǐ	shuō	nǐ	hái	bú	è.
	刚	才	你	说	你	还	不	饿。

Wáng Péng: Gāng cái què shí bú è, xiàn zài shì
王 朋: 刚 才 确 实 不 饿, 现 在 是

yǒu xiē jī è gǎn le.
有 些 饥 饿 感 了。

Zhāng Lì: Jīn tiān gěi nǐ jiàn xíng.
张 丽: 今 天 给 你 饯 行。

Wáng Péng: Tài xiè xie nǐ le.
王 朋: 太 谢 谢 你 了。

Zhāng Lì: Zhè ge fàn guǎn de jiǎo zi hé hún tún
张 丽: 这 个 饭 馆 的 饺 子 和 馄 饨

dōu fēi cháng hǎo chī.
都 非 常 好 吃。

Nǐ xiǎng chī shén me xiàn de?
你 想 吃 什 么 馅 的?

Wáng Péng: Chī jī ròu xiàn de hún tún ba.
王 朋: 吃 鸡 肉 馅 的 馄 饨 吧。

Zhāng Lì: Hǎo de. Zhǔ shí yào bú yào zài diǎn
张 丽: 好 的。 主 食 要 不 要 再 点

yí ge ròu jiā mó huò zhě mán tou,
一 个 肉 夹 馍 或 者 馒 头,

huò zhě yù mǐ bǐng?
或 者 玉 米 饼?

Wáng Péng: Yào yí ge yù mǐ bǐng ba. Yì wǎn
王 朋: 要 一 个 玉 米 饼 吧。 一 碗

hún tún wǒ jiù jī běn shàng chī bǎo le.
馄 饨 我 就 基 本 上 吃 饱 了。

Zhāng	Lì:	Hái	yào	diǎn	shén	me	yǐn	liào?
张	丽:	还	要	点	什	么	饮	料?

Wáng	Péng:	Yǒu	hún	tún	tāng	le,	jiù	bú	yào	yǐn
王	朋:	有	馄	饨	汤	了,	就	不	要	饮

liào	le.
料	了。

VOCABULARY

饥饿感 jī'è gǎn	(feeling of) hunger
饯行 jiànxíng	to see someone off, to say farewell to someone
饺子 jiǎozi	dumpling
馄饨 húntún	wonton
馅 xiàn	dumpling filling
主食 zhǔshí	staple food
肉夹馍 ròujiāmó	pancake filled with meat
馒头 mántou	steamed bun
玉米饼 yùmǐbǐng	corn cake
吃饱 chībǎo	to eat until full
饮料 yǐnliào	drinks

COMPREHENSION QUESTIONS

Answer the following questions in English.

I. Where do the two friends seem to be?

✎_____

_____

2. Is Wang Peng hungry?

3. Why did Zhang Li offer to treat Wang Peng to a meal?

4. What type of meat did they order in their wontons?

5. What did they order for their staple food?

6. What drinks did they order?

* * *

Once you're happy with your answers, turn to page 176 to check them.

36

翻译挑战 4
Fānyì tiǎozhàn 4
TRANSLATION CHALLENGE

In this Translation Challenge, we're focusing on translating question words, like *what?*, *who?*, *where?* and so on. Your task is to translate each question below into Chinese. Answers will be provided both in characters and in pinyin, so you can choose how to write your translation. If you need help, you can turn to the end of this section to find some hints.

* * *

1. What do you do for a living?

✎ _____

_____

_____

2. Where do you play tennis?

   _____

   _____

   _____

3. When do you go to work every day?

   _____

   _____

   _____

4. Who helps you learn Chinese?

   _____

   _____

   _____

5. Which book do you like better?

   _____

   _____

   _____

6. How many dogs do you have?

   _____

   _____

   _____

HINTS

If you need some help, you may find the following hints useful.

1. In sentence 1, use 什么 **shénme** to ask the question.

2. In sentence 2, use 哪里 **nǎlǐ** to ask the question.

3. You can use either 什么时候 **shénme shíhou** or 几点 **jǐdiǎn** in sentence 3.

4. In sentence 4, use 谁 **shéi** to ask *who?*

5. Use 哪 **nǎ** to help you translate sentence 5.

6. To ask *how many?* use either 几 **jǐ** or 多少 **duōshǎo** followed by the appropriate measure word.

* * *

Once you're happy with your translations, turn to pages 177-178 to find our suggested answers.

37

聂华苓
Niè Huálíng

FAMOUS CHINESE SPEAKERS

In this activity, you will practise your reading skills while learning a little about 聂华苓 **Niè Huálíng**. Known in English as Hualing Nieh Engle, she is a writer who is well known across the world. Use the vocabulary list to help you as you read through the text, then answer the comprehension questions on the next page to test your understanding. If you'd like an extra challenge, why not try reading the text and answering the questions before looking at the vocabulary list? Remember, it's always there if you need it.

* * *

Niè	Huá	líng	shì	shì	jiè	shàng	yǒu	míng	de	zuò	jiā.
聂	华	苓	是	世	界	上	有	名	的	作	家。

Tā	1925	nián	zài	Zhōng	guó	chū	shēng,	1949	nián	bān	dào
她	1925	年	在	中	国	出	生,	1949	年	搬	到

Tái	wān,	1964	nián	bān	dào	Měi	guó	Ài	hé	huá,	2024
台	湾,	1964	年	搬	到	美	国	爱	荷	华,	2024

年10月21日逝世，活了将近一百岁。聂华苓一生在中国、台湾和美国都写了很多书。聂华苓1967年在爱荷华创立了国际写作计划。这个计划帮助150个国家的1400名作家来美国写作，和其他作者交流。文学界很多人说，聂华苓是"世界文学组织之母"。她自己说，"我是一棵树，根在大陆，干在台湾，叶在爱荷华"。人们补充说，"聂华苓的文学果实在全世界"。

143

VOCABULARY

作家 zuòjiā	writer
出生 chūshēng	to be born
搬到 bāndào	to move to
台湾 Táiwān	Taiwan
爱荷华 Àihéhuá	Iowa
逝世 shìshì	to die
一生 yìshēng	lifetime
创立 chuànglì	to establish, to found
国际写作计划 Guójì Xiězuò Jìhuà	The International Writing Program
写作 xiězuò	to write
交流 jiāoliú	to interact
文学界 wénxuéjiè	the literary world
世界文学组织之母 Shìjiè Wénxué Zǔzhī zhī Mǔ	Mother of World Literature Organisation
根 gēn	root
大陆 dàlù	mainland
干 gàn	branch
叶 yè	leaf
补充 bǔchōng	to add
果实 guǒshí	fruit

COMPREHENSION QUESTIONS

Answer the following questions in English.

I. When was Hualing Nieh Engle born and when did she die?

✎ _____

_____

2. What did she establish in 1967 in Iowa?

   ✎ _____

   _____

3. How many writers benefited from the programme?

   ✎ _____

   _____

4. What do writers across the world call Hualing Nieh Engle?

   ✎ _____

   _____

5. If we compare Hualing Nieh Engle to a tree, where are her roots? Where are her branches?

   ✎ _____

   _____

6. Where are her leaves? Where are her fruits?

   ✎ _____

   _____

* * *

Once you're happy with your answers, you can check them on page 178.

38

复合量词
Fùhé liàngcí
FOR GOOD MEASURE

In this activity, we'll practise using 复合量词 **fùhé liàngcí** – compound measure words. Look at the explanation and the examples below, then it's over to you in the exercises. 加油! **Jiāyóu!**

* * *

Compound measure words are made up of two or more words. Let's look at some examples of compound measure words:

Xuéxiào de zhǔ xiàoqū hé fēnxiào zhījiān de xiàochē měitiān yǒu èrshí ge chēcì.

学校的主校区和分校之间的校车每天有二十个车次。

Each day, there are 20 shuttle bus journeys between the main campus and the branch campus.

Liǎng ge guójiā zhījiān de hángbān měizhōu xiànzài zhǐyǒu sānshí ge jiàcì le.

两个国家之间的航班每周现在只有三十个架次了。

The number of flights between the two countries has now been reduced to 30 flights a week.

Zhè tiáo hé shàng de dùchuán měitiān zhǐyǒu wǔ ge chuáncì.

这条河上的渡船每天只有五个船次。

There are only five ferry journeys a day between the two banks of the river.

Zhè ge bówùguǎn měinián lái cānguān de rén yǒu wǔshí wàn réncì.

这个博物馆每年来参观的人有五十万人次。

This museum entertains 500,000 visitors each year.

Note that it sounds most natural to include 个 **ge** between a number and the compound measure words 车次 **chēcì**, 架次 **jiàcì** and 船次 **chuáncì**.

Compound measure words can also be reduplicated measure words, such as 个个 **gègè**. In this case, it means *everyone is included and there's no exception.*

Another example is 一个一个 **yí ge yí ge**. In this case, it means *one by one in good order.* Let's look at some examples:

Lǎoshī gègè dōu hěn hǎo.

老师个个都很好。 *Every one of the teachers is good.*

Dōngtiān tiāntiān dōu shì yīntiān.

冬天天天都是阴天。 *In winter, every day is cloudy.*

Tā xiě de shū běnběn dōu shì hǎo shū.

她写的书本本都是好书。 *Every one of the books she wrote is good.*

Zhème duō shū, wǒ yào yì běn yì běn kàn.

这么多书，我要一本一本看。 *There are so many books, I'll read them one by one.*

Rìzi yì tiān yì tiān guòqù le, kěshì tā háishì méi yǒu shōudào huíxìn.

日子一天一天过去了，可是她还是没有收到回信。 *One day after another has passed, but she still hasn't heard back.*

Lǎoshī yào wǒmen yí ge yí ge jiǎnghuà.

老师要我们一个一个讲话。 *The teacher asked us to talk one by one.*

EXERCISE 1 - MATCH

Draw a line to match each Chinese phrase with its English translation.

十人次	*10 flights*
二十个架次	*100 flights*
五个船次	*30 people visiting / participating*
五十个车次	*50 bus journeys*
十个架次	*5 ship journeys*
五个车次	*5 bus journeys*
三十人次	*10 people visiting / participating*
二十个船次	*20 ship journeys*
一百个架次	*20 flights*

EXERCISE 2 - FILL IN THE GAPS

Complete the following sentences by adding in the reduplicated measure words, using the hints in English to help you.

Note that if 不是 **bú shì** is placed before 个个 **gègè**, it is "partial negation", which means *not every one*. If 不是 **bú shì** is placed before the verb, it is "total negation", which means *every one is not*.

1. 这里的老师不是 ✎_____ 都很好。 **Zhèlǐ de lǎoshī bú shì ✎_____ dōu hěn hǎo.**
   (each and every one)

2. 上课了，学生 ✎_____ 走进了教室。
   Shàngkè le, xuésheng ✎_____ zǒujìn le jiàoshì. *(one by one)*

3. 这里的冬天天气很不好，✎_____ 都是 阴天。 **Zhèlǐ de dōngtiān tiānqì hěn bù hǎo, ✎_____ dōu shì yīntiān.** *(each and every day)*

4. 她写的书 ✎_____ 都是好书。 **Tā xiě de shū ✎_____ dōu shì hǎo shū.**
   (each and every one)

5. 这么多书，我只能 ✎_____ 地看。
   Zhème duō shū, wǒ zhǐnéng ✎_____ de kàn.
   (one book at a time)

6. 日子 ✎_____ 过去了，她的身体慢慢好 起来了。 **Rìzi ✎_____ guòqù le, tā de shēntǐ mànmàn hǎo qǐlái le.** *(one day after another)*

7. 她去中国去了很多次，✎_____ 都去北京。
   Tā qù Zhōngguó qù le hěn duō cì, ✎_____ dōu
   qù Běijīng. *(each and every time)*

8. 他是足球迷，只要有比赛，他 ✎_____
   都要看。 Tā shì zúqiúmí, zhǐyào yǒu bǐsài, tā
   ✎_____ dōu yào kàn. *(each and every game)*

9. 我们不要一起说话，要 ✎_____ 地讲话。
   Wǒmen bú yào yìqǐ shuōhuà, yào ✎_____
   de jiǎnghuà. *(one person at a time)*

10. 哥哥 ✎_____ 都要喝咖啡，不喝咖啡就
    不能工作。 Gēge ✎_____ dōu yào hē kāfēi,
    bù hē kāfēi jiù bù néng gōngzuò. *(each and every day)*

* * *

太棒了! **Tài bàng le!** When you're ready, you'll find the answers
on pages 179-180.

39

成千上万
Chéng qiān shàng wàn
NUMBER FOCUS

There are many four-word idioms in Chinese that are based on the characters 千 **qiān** (*a thousand*) and 万 **wàn** (*ten thousand*). In this Number Focus activity, we are going to learn some of these idioms and practise using them in context. 开始吧! **Kāishǐ ba!**

* * *

成千上万   **chéng qiān shàng wàn**

LITERAL TRANSLATION: *to reach a thousand and rise to ten thousand*
IDIOMATIC TRANSLATION: *thousands upon thousands of*

千言万语   **qiān yán wàn yǔ**

LITERAL TRANSLATION: *a thousand words and ten thousand phrases*
IDIOMATIC TRANSLATION: *endless words to say, having a lot to say*

万里挑一   **wàn lǐ tiāo yī**

LITERAL TRANSLATION: *pick one out of ten thousand*
IDIOMATIC TRANSLATION: *one in a million, a rare find*

千真万确　　　**qiān zhēn wàn què**

LITERAL TRANSLATION: *a thousand times true and ten thousand times certain*

IDIOMATIC TRANSLATION: *absolutely certain, undeniably true*

气象万千　　　**qì xiàng wàn qiān**

LITERAL TRANSLATION: *ten thousand kinds of appearances or phenomena*

IDIOMATIC TRANSLATION: *a magnificent and varied scene, a grand spectacle*

千头万绪　　　**qiān tóu wàn xù**

LITERAL TRANSLATION: *a thousand loose ends and ten thousand strands*

IDIOMATIC TRANSLATION: *chaos, too many things to tackle*

千丝万缕　　　**qiān sī wàn lǚ**

LITERAL TRANSLATION: *a thousand threads and ten thousand fine strands*

IDIOMATIC TRANSLATION: *closely related in many areas, intertwined, inextricably linked*

万水千山　　　**wàn shuǐ qiān shān**

LITERAL TRANSLATION: *ten thousand rivers and a thousand mountains*

IDIOMATIC TRANSLATION: *a long and arduous journey, through countless hardships*

一字千金　　　**yí zì qiān jīn**

LITERAL TRANSLATION: *one word is worth a thousand gold pieces*

IDIOMATIC TRANSLATION: *every word is priceless, words of huge value*

万马奔腾　　　**wàn mǎ bēn téng**

LITERAL TRANSLATION: *ten thousand horses galloping*

IDIOMATIC TRANSLATION: *an unstoppable force, with great momentum*

EXERCISE 1 - TRANSLATE

Can you remember what the following idioms mean? Write down the idiomatic translation of each one.

1. 千言万语 qiān yán wàn yǔ

   🖉_____

2. 万马奔腾 wàn mǎ bēn téng

   🖉_____

3. 万水千山 wàn shuǐ qiān shān

   🖉_____

4. 气象万千 qì xiàng wàn qiān

   🖉_____

5. 一字千金 yí zì qiān jīn

   🖉_____

EXERCISE 2 - FILL IN THE GAPS

Fill in each of the gaps with one of the idioms we've learned, according to the context.

1. 从北京出发,他们走了很多天, 走过了
   🖉_____, 最后才走到南京。
   Cóng Běijīng chūfā, tāmen zǒu le hěn duō tiān, zǒu guò le
   🖉_____ , **zuìhòu cái zǒu dào Nánjīng.**

2. 你帮了我一个大忙, 我有 _____ ,
   可是只能说一句"谢谢你"。　**Nǐ bāng le wǒ yí ge dà
   máng, wǒ yǒu** _____ **, kěshì
   zhǐnéng shuō yí jù "xièxie nǐ".**

3. 你的书不在我这里, _____ 。
   不信你可以自己找一找。　**Nǐ de shū bú zài wǒ zhèlǐ,**
   _____ **. Bú xìn nǐ kěyǐ zìjǐ zhǎo yì
   zhǎo.**

4. 体育场里有很多人, _____
   的人在一起喊, "加油"!　**Tǐyùchǎng lǐ yǒu hěn duō rén,**
   _____ **de rén zài yìqǐ hǎn, "jiāyóu"!**

5. 这个运动员非常非常厉害, 是我们
   _____ 选出来的。　**Zhè ge
   yùndòngyuán fēicháng fēicháng lìhai, shì wǒmen**
   _____ **xuǎn chūlái de.**

* * *

You can find the answers to both exercises on pages 181-182.

40

面条
Miàntiáo
TASTE BUD TANTALISER

面条 **miàntiáo** (*noodles*) are one of the most important elements of Chinese cuisine. Use the vocabulary list to help you as you learn how to make 面条 **miàntiáo** in the recipe below, then complete the exercise that follows.

* * *

But first, an interesting cultural fact: did you know that in China it is customary to eat noodles on your birthday? When it is someone's birthday in China, you can say to them: 长命百岁! **cháng mìng bǎi suì!** This means *may you live to be 100!* and is a way of wishing someone a long life. As noodles are known for their length, they signify a long life and so are considered appropriate and lucky to eat on a birthday. Now, let's find out how you can make 面条 **miàntiáo**.

Cái liào
材 料

miàn fěn liǎng bàng
面 粉 两 磅

jī dàn yí ge
鸡 蛋 一 个

qīng shuǐ yì shēng
清 水 一 升

Zuò fǎ
做 法

(一) Bǎ liǎng bàng miàn fàng dào yí ge pén lǐ, zài
把 两 磅 面 放 到 一 个 盆 里, 再

bǎ yí ge jī dàn dǎ dào pén lǐ.
把 一 个 鸡 蛋 打 到 盆 里。

(二) Wǎng miàn shàng dào yì xiē shuǐ. Yì biān dào shuǐ,
往 面 上 倒 一 些 水。 一 边 倒 水,

yì biān yòng kuài zi jiǎo bàn, zhí dào bàn yún.
一 边 用 筷 子 搅 拌, 直 到 拌 匀。

(三) Zài pén lǐ yòng shǒu huó miàn, zhí dào miàn hé
在 盆 里 用 手 和 面, 直 到 面 和

shuǐ wán quán zài yì qǐ, huó chéng yí ge miàn
水 完 全 在 一 起, 和 成 一 个 面

tuán.
团。

(四) Zài àn bǎn shàng sǎ yì xiē gān miàn fěn, rán
在 案 板 上 撒 一 些 干 面 粉, 然

hòu bǎ miàn tuán fàng zài shàng miàn. Yòng gǎn miàn
后 把 面 团 放 在 上 面。 用 擀 面

zhàng fǎn fù gǎn, zhí dào gǎn báo.
杖 反 复 擀, 直 到 擀 薄。

(五)
Bǎ	báo	báo	de	miàn	zhé	dié	qǐ	lái,	yòng	dāo
把	薄	薄	的	面	折	叠	起	来,	用	刀

qiē	chéng	cháng	cháng	de	miàn	tiáo.
切	成	长	长	的	面	条。

(六)
Yòng	dà	guō	shāo	kāi	shuǐ	hòu,	bǎ	miàn	tiáo	fàng
用	大	锅	烧	开	水	后,	把	面	条	放

jìn	qù	zhǔ	shí	wǔ	fēn	zhōng,	lāo	chū	lái	yǐ
进	去	煮	十	五	分	钟,	捞	出	来	以

hòu	jiù	kě	yǐ	chī	le.
后	就	可	以	吃	了。

(七)
Miàn	tiáo	shì	zhǔ	shí,	chī	de	shí	hòu	dāng	rán
面	条	是	主	食,	吃	的	时	候	当	然

hái	kě	yǐ	chī	nǐ	xǐ	huān	de	cài.
还	可	以	吃	你	喜	欢	的	菜。

VOCABULARY

面粉 miànfěn	*flour*
升 shēng	*litre*
做法 zuòfǎ	*method*
盆 pén	*bowl, basin*
倒水 dàoshuǐ	*to pour water*
搅拌 jiǎobàn	*to stir*
拌匀 bànyún	*well mixed*
和面 huómiàn	*to make a dough*
面团 miàntuán	*a piece of dough*
案板 ànbǎn	*chopping board*

撒 sǎ	*to sprinkle*
擀面杖 gǎnmiànzhàng	*rolling pin*
反复擀 fǎnfù gǎn	*to roll repeatedly*
薄薄的 báobáode	*very thin*
折叠 zhédié	*to fold*
切成 qiē chéng	*to cut (something) into*
煮 zhǔ	*to cook by boiling*
捞出来 lāo chūlái	*to remove from water*

COMPREHENSION QUESTIONS

Answer the following questions. Except for question 1, give your answers in English.

1. Today is your Chinese friend's birthday. What could you say to them?

   ✎ _____

   _____

2. When you make the dough, do you add the water into the flour or add the flour into the water?

   ✎ _____

   _____

3. Before you roll out the dough, what do you sprinkle on the board?

   ✎ _____

   _____

4. Before you cut the dough into noodles, what do you need to do?

5. For how long do you need to boil the noodles before you can eat them?

* * *

When you're ready, you can find the answers on page 182.

ANSWERS
10-MINUTE COFFEE BREAKS

21. 翻译挑战 1 Fānyì tiǎozhàn 1
TRANSLATION CHALLENGE

1. 我今天打扫房间了。 **Wǒ jīntiān dǎsǎo fángjiān le.**
   or
   今天我打扫房间了。 **Jīntiān wǒ dǎsǎo fángjiān le.**

   EXPLANATION:

   - In this sentence, 了 **le** is needed to indicate the completion of the action.
   - 今天 **jīntiān**, an adverb of time, can either be placed before the verb, 打扫 **dǎsǎo**, or at the beginning of the sentence.

2. 她买了三张电影票。 **Tā mǎi le sān zhāng diànyǐng piào.**

   EXPLANATION:

   - Whenever we are referring to a quantity of something within a completed action sentence, 了 **le** should be placed before the quantity.

- In this sentence, the measure word 张 **zhāng** is needed between the quantity (三 **sān**) and the object (电影票 **diànyǐng piào**). 张 **zhāng** is the measure word that is used for flat objects.

3. 我弟弟看了很多书。 **Wǒ dìdi kàn le hěnduō shū.**

EXPLANATION:

- In this sentence, 了 **le** is still placed before 很多 **hěnduō**, even though 很多 **hěnduō** is not an exact quantity.

4. 她妈妈给我们做饭了。 **Tā māma gěi wǒmen zuòfàn le.**

EXPLANATION:

- 了 **le** should be placed at the end of the sentence to indicate that the action of cooking is done and the food is ready for us to eat.
- Remember to place 给我们 **gěi wǒmen** (*for us*) before the verb.

5. 她已经洗衣服了。 **Tā yǐjīng xǐ yīfu le.**

EXPLANATION:

- The adverb 已经 **yǐjīng** (*already*) should be placed before the verb.
- Remember to add 了 **le** at the end of the sentence to indicate that the action is complete.

22. 孔子 Kǒngzǐ
FAMOUS CHINESE SPEAKERS

1. Confucius was a great thinker, statesman and educator.
2. He was born in 551 BCE and died in 479 BCE.
3. He taught over 3,000 students and 72 of them became famous.
4. That everyone has the right to education, no matter who they are.
5. Don't do to others what you don't want others to do to you.

23. 独体和集体量词 Dútǐ hé jítǐ liàngcí
FOR GOOD MEASURE

EXERCISE 1 – MATCH

一条鱼 yì tiáo yú	– a fish
两个妹妹 liǎng ge mèimei	– two younger sisters
三双鞋子 sān shuāng xiézi	– three pairs of shoes
一群工人 yì qún gōngrén	– a group of workers
三条领带 sāntiáo lǐngdài	– three ties
十张桌子 shí zhāng zhuōzi	– ten tables
两个朋友 liǎng ge péngyou	– two friends
四双筷子 sì shuāng kuàizi	– four pairs of chopsticks
五张红纸 wǔ zhāng hóng zhǐ	– five pieces of red paper
一打鸡蛋 yì dá jīdàn	– a dozen eggs

EXERCISE 2 – FILL IN THE GAPS

1. 爸爸今天买了三**条**围巾。 Bàba jīntiān mǎi le sān **tiáo** wéijīn.

   TRANSLATION: *Dad bought three scarves today.*

2. 我们是六**个**人，为什么只给我们五**双**筷子？ Wǒmen shì liù **ge** rén, wèishénme zhǐ gěi wǒmen wǔ **shuāng** kuàizi?

   TRANSLATION: *There are six of us – why have we only been given five pairs of chopsticks?*

3. 她有两**张**电影票。 Tā yǒu liǎng **zhāng** diànyǐngpiào.

   TRANSLATION: *She has two cinema tickets.*

4. 妹妹今天穿了一**条**白裙子，很漂亮。 Mèimei jīntiān chuān le yì **tiáo** bái qúnzi, hěn piàoliang.

   TRANSLATION: *My younger sister is wearing a white skirt today. She looks so beautiful.*

5. 一打玫瑰花多少钱? Yì **dá** méiguīhuā duōshǎo qián?

TRANSLATION: *How much does a dozen roses cost?*

6. 他家有一大群山羊。 Tā jiā yǒu yí dà **qún** shānyáng.

TRANSLATION: *His family owns a large herd of goats.*

7. 我有很多双鞋。你挑一双吧。 Wǒ yǒu hěn duō **shuāng** xié. Nǐ tiāo yì **shuāng** ba.

TRANSLATION: *I have many pairs of shoes. Why don't you choose a pair.*

8. 一张白纸也很好。你想画什么, 就画什么。 Yì **zhāng** bái zhǐ yě hěn hǎo. Nǐ xiǎng huà shénme, jiù huà shénme.

TRANSLATION: *A blank piece of paper is also very good. You can draw anything you want.*

9. 你的房间里有几张床? Nǐ de fángjiān lǐ yǒu jǐ **zhāng** chuáng?

TRANSLATION: *How many beds are there in your room?*

10. 今天商店的鸡蛋很便宜, 妈妈买了两打。 够我们吃十天了。 Jīntiān shāngdiàn de jīdàn hěn piányi, māma mǎi le liǎng **dá**. Gòu wǒmen chī shí tiān le.

TRANSLATION: *The eggs in the shop are very cheap today, so mum bought two dozen, which will last us for ten days.*

24. 重要年份 Zhòngyào niánfèn
NUMBER FOCUS

DATES

1. *221 BCE* 公元前二二一年 **gōngyuánqián èr èr yī nián**

2. *206 BCE* 公元前二零六年 **gōngyuánqián èr líng liù nián**

3. *220* CE 公元二二零年 gōngyuán èr èr líng nián

4. *618* CE 公元六一八年 gōngyuán liù yī bā nián

5. *1206* CE 公元一二零六年 gōngyuán yī ér líng liù nián

6. *1368* CE 公元一三六八年 gōngyuán yī sān liù bā nián

7. *1911* CE 公元一九一一年 gōngyuán yī jiǔ yīyī nián

8. *1949* CE 公元一九四九年 gōngyuán yī jiǔ sì jiǔ nián

IMPORTANT EVENTS

1. 秦国在公元前二二一年统一了中国。 Qínguó zài gōngyuánqián **èr èr yī** nián tǒngyī le Zhōngguó.

2. 汉朝在公元前二零六年建立。 Hàncháo zài gōngyuánqián **èr líng liù** nián jiànlì.

3. 汉朝在公元二二零年结束。 Hàncháo zài gōngyuán **èr èr líng** nián jiéshù.

4. 唐朝在公元六一八年建立。 Tángcháo zài gōngyuán **liù yī bā** nián jiànlì.

5. 元朝在公元一二零六年建立。 Yuáncháo zài gōngyuán **yī èr líng liù** nián jiànlì.

6. 明朝在公元一三六八年建立。 Míngcháo zài gōngyuán **yī sān liù bā** nián jiànlì.

7. 中华民国在一九一一年建立。 Zhōnghuá Mínguó zài **yī jiǔ yī yī** nián jiànlì.

8. 中华人民共和国在一九四九年建立。 Zhōnghuá Rénmín Gònghéguó zài **yī jiǔ sì jiǔ** nián jiànlì.

25. 番茄鸡蛋 Fānqié jīdàn
TASTE BUD TANTALISER

1. 不对 – You need two tomatoes and three eggs.

2. 不对 – 葱花 are chopped green onions.

3. 对

4. 不对 – The eggs should be stir-fried first and the tomatoes should be stir-fried second.

5. 对

26. 翻译挑战 2 Fānyì tiǎozhàn 2
TRANSLATION CHALLENGE

1. 我可以坐在这里吗？Wǒ kěyǐ zuòzài zhèlǐ ma?
   or
   我能坐在这里吗？Wǒ néng zuòzài zhèlǐ ma?
   or
   我可以不可以/能不能坐在这里？Wǒ kěyǐ bù kěyǐ / néng bù néng zuòzài zhèli?

   EXPLANATION:

- You can use 可以 kěyǐ to talk about having permission to do something.

- 能 néng also means *to have permission* to do something, but also means *to be able* to do something.

- You can form the question by using 吗 ma, or by using 可以不可以 kěyǐ bù kěyǐ or 能不能 néng bù néng.

- Note that you can also translate *here* as 这儿 zhè'er, which is slightly less formal than 这里 zhèlǐ.

2. 学生应该上课以前交作文。 **Xuéshēng yīnggāi shàngkè yǐqián jiāo zuòwén.**

   or

   学生得上课以前交作文。 **Xuéshēng děi shàngkè yǐqián jiāo zuòwén.**

   EXPLANATION:

- Both 应该 **yīnggāi** and 得 **děi** express being obligated to do something.

3. 你觉得他今天会来吗? **Nǐ juéde tā jīntiān huì lái ma?**

   or

   你觉得他今天能来吗? **Nǐ juéde tā jīntiān néng lái ma?**

   or

   他觉得不觉得他今天会/能来? **Nǐ juéde bù juéde tā jīntiān huì / néng lái?**

   EXPLANATION:

- We use 会 **huì** to talk about something we expect will happen in the future. In other contexts, 会 **huì** can also translate as *can* or *to be able to*.
- 能 **néng** means *to be able to* and it also works in this context.
- You can form the question by using 吗 **ma** or by using 觉得 不觉得 **juéde bù juéde**.

4. 她想去游泳, 不想去买东西。 **Tā xiǎng qù yóuyǒng, bù xiǎng qù mǎi dōngxi.**

   or

   她要去游泳, 不要去买东西。 **Tā yào qù yóuyǒng, bù yào qù mǎi dōngxi.**

   EXPLANATION:

- You can use either 想 **xiǎng** or 要 **yào** to express wanting to do something.

- Note that it is more natural in Chinese to repeat 想去 **xiǎng qù** or 要去 **yào qù** in the second part of the sentence, whereas in the English sentence *wants to go* only appears in the first part.

5. 我们早饭以后得打扫房间。 **Wǒmen zǎofàn yǐhòu děi dǎsǎo fángjiān.**

   or

   我们早饭以后必须打扫房间。 **Wǒmen zǎofàn yǐhòu bìxū dǎsǎo fángjiān.**

   EXPLANATION:

- 必须 **bìxū** and 得 **děi** both mean *to have to do (something)*.

27. 三毛 Sān Máo
FAMOUS CHINESE SPEAKERS

1. San Mao was born in 1943 and died in 1991.

2. The first title mentioned in the text, 《撒哈拉的故事》, refers to the Sahara Desert. The last title in the list, 《亲爱的三毛》, includes her name.

3. Yes, she did live in Africa.

4. Her books transport her readers to Africa and the Americas, and to deserts and forests, where not so many people get the chance to go.

5. She joked that her books were not very good and were only worth three dimes (三毛 **sān máo** = *three dimes*).

28. 临时量词 Línshí liàngcí
FOR GOOD MEASURE

EXERCISE 1 - MATCH

三篮桃子 **sān lán táozi**	– *three baskets of peaches*
一屋烟 **yì wū yān**	– *a house (full) of smoke*
两勺醋 **liǎng sháo cù**	– *two spoonfuls of vinegar*
四袋红薯 **sì dài hóngshǔ**	– *four bags of sweet potatoes*
两卡车石头 **liǎng kǎchē shítou**	– *two truckloads of rocks*
一船新汽车 **yì chuán xīn qìchē**	– *a shipload of new cars*
三碗汤 **sān wǎn tāng**	– *three bowls of soup*
五瓶酒 **wǔ píng jiǔ**	– *five bottles of wine*
一桌信 **yì zhuō xìn**	– *a table (full) of letters*
十箱衣服 **shí xiāng yīfú**	– *ten boxes of clothes*

EXERCISE 2 - FILL IN THE GAPS

1. 爸爸今天买了一**瓶**酱油。 Bàba jīntiān mǎi le yì **píng** jiàngyóu.

   TRANSLATION: *Dad bought a bottle of soy sauce today.*

2. 我们是六个人，为什么只给我们五**碗汤**？Wǒmen shì liù ge rén, wèishénme zhǐ gěi wǒmen wǔ **wǎn** tāng?

   TRANSLATION: *There are six of us, why have we only been given five bowls of soup?*

3. 屋子里有三箱书。 Wūzi lǐ yǒu **sān** xiāng shū.

   TRANSLATION: *There are three boxes of books in the room.*

4. 你不是想看报纸吗？这里有一桌报纸。Nǐ bú shì xiǎng kàn bàozhǐ ma? Zhèlǐ yǒu yì **zhuō** bàozhǐ.

TRANSLATION: *Don't you want to read a newspaper? Here is a table full of newspapers.*

5. 两卡车土一共要多少钱？Liǎng **kǎchē** tǔ yígòng yào duōshǎo qián?

TRANSLATION: *How much do two truckloads of dirt cost in total?*

6. 学生给老师送去了三篮苹果。Xuésheng gěi lǎoshī sòngqù le sān **lán** píngguǒ.

TRANSLATION: *The students gave the teacher three baskets of apples.*

7. 我只要用两勺油。Wǒ zhǐyào yòng liǎng **sháo** yóu.

TRANSLATION: *I'm only going to use two spoonfuls of oil.*

8. 学校这个冬天要买四袋土豆。Xuéxiào zhège dōngtiān yào mǎi sì **dài** tǔdòu.

TRANSLATION: *The school will buy four bags of potatoes this winter.*

9. 我们会有更多的新汽车。明天会来一船新汽车。Wǒmen huì yǒu gèng duō de xīn qìchē. Míngtiān huì lái yì **chuán** xīn qìchē.

TRANSLATION: *We're going to have more new cars. A shipload of new cars is coming tomorrow.*

10. 家里有一屋人在等你。你快回来吧。Jiālǐ yǒu yì **wū** rén zài děng nǐ. Nǐ kuài huílái ba.

TRANSLATION: *There is a house full of people waiting for you at home. Come back soon.*

29. 现在几点? Xiànzài jǐdiǎn?
NUMBER FOCUS

EXERCISE 1 - WRITE IN DIGITS

1. 9:00 AM

2. 8:05 PM

3. 3:45

4. 11:00

5. 4:30

6. 4:00 AM

7. 22:00

8. 2:00 PM

EXERCISE 2 - WRITE IN CHINESE

1. 下午三点 xiàwǔ sān diǎn

2. 下午两点半 xiàwǔ liǎng diǎn bàn

3. 上午九点四十五 shàngwǔ jiǔ diǎn sìshíwǔ or
   差一刻上午十点 chà yí kè shàngwǔ shí diǎn

4. 凌晨两点一刻 língchén liǎng diǎn yí kè

5. 上午十一点 shàngwǔ shíyī diǎn

6. 晚上九点半 wǎnshàng jiǔ diǎn bàn

7. 上午八点 shàngwǔ bā diǎn

8. 下午五点四十五 xiàwǔ wǔ diǎn sìshíwǔ or
   差一刻下午六点 chà yí kè xiàwǔ liù diǎn

30. 包饺子 Bāo jiǎozi
TASTE BUD TANTALISER

1. One pound.
2. Two spoonfuls.
3. Cooking oil, salt, soy sauce and ginger powder.
4. One.
5. False – you put the dumplings in after the water is boiling.
6. 10 minutes.

31. 翻译挑战 3 Fānyì tiǎozhàn 3
TRANSLATION CHALLENGE

1. 她说阿拉伯语吗? Tā shuō Ālābóyǔ ma?

   EXPLANATION:

   • Remember that you can form the question by using 吗 ma or 说不说 shuō bù shuō: 她说不说阿拉伯语? tā shuō bù shuō Ālābóyǔ?

2. 他在这里没有朋友, 对吗? Tā zài zhèli méi yǒu péngyou, duì ma?

   EXPLANATION:

   • As an alternative to 对吗? duì ma?, you can also use 是吗? shì ma? to ask a confirmative question like this, in which you're asking for confirmation of a fact.

   • You can also translate *here* as 这儿 zhè'er, which is slightly less formal than 这里 zhèlǐ.

3. 你是不是法国人? Nǐ shì bú shì Fǎguórén?

   EXPLANATION:

   • You are probably already familiar with this very common way of structuring a question in Chinese, using the positive form followed by the negative form of the verb: 你是不是 **nǐ shì bú shì** (literally *are you or aren't you*).

- Of course, you can also form the question by using 吗 **ma** instead: 你是法国人吗? **nǐ shì Fǎguórén ma?**

4. 你有没有手电? **Nǐ yǒu méi yǒu shǒudiàn?**

EXPLANATION:

- Like in sentence 3, we have the positive form followed by the negative form, but this time with the verb 有 **yǒu.** This is a very common way of structuring the question when asking if someone has something.
- Of course, you can also form the question by using 吗 **ma** instead: 你有手电吗? **nǐ yǒu shǒudiàn ma?**

5. 你要喝咖啡还是茶? **Nǐ yào hē kāfēi háishì chá?**

EXPLANATION:

- Use 还是 **háishì** between the two objects to ask a question in which you are offering alternatives.

6. 你还是你的女朋友会去美国? **Nǐ háishì nǐ de nǚpéngyou huì qù Měiguó?**

EXPLANATION:

- In this sentence, we can use 还是 **háishì** again and it is placed between *you* and *your girlfriend* to show two alternative subjects.
- *Or* is always translated as 还是 **háishì** in questions expressing alternatives, but when you use *or* in a statement, it will be translated as 或者 **huòzhě**: for example, in the statement 我或者我的女朋友会去美国 **wǒ huòzhě wǒ de nǚpéngyou huì qù Měiguó** (*I or my girlfriend will go to the USA*).

32. 庄子 Zhuāngzǐ
FAMOUS CHINESE SPEAKERS

1. By a river.
2. A school of fish.
3. Swimming freely to and fro.
4. How happy they are!
5. You are not the fish, how can you know that they are happy?
6. You are not me, how can you know that I don't know that the fish are happy?

33. 动作量词 Dòngzuò liàngcí
FOR GOOD MEASURE

EXERCISE 1 - MATCH

闻一下	wén yí xià	– to sniff briefly
打两场	dǎ liǎng chǎng	– to play two games
踢一脚	tī yì jiǎo	– to kick once
切一刀	qiē yì dāo	– to make a cut with a knife
去两次	qù liǎng cì	– to go twice
砍三斧	kǎn sān fǔ	– to cut three times with an axe
咬一口	yǎo yì kǒu	– to take a bite
看三遍	kàn sān biàn	– to read three times
听一下	tīng yí xià	– to listen briefly
写十遍	xiě shí biàn	– to write ten times

EXERCISE 2 - FILL IN THE GAPS

1. 爸爸今天看了**两场**篮球赛。Bàba jīntiān kàn le **liǎng chǎng** lánqiú sài.

   TRANSLATION: *Dad watched two basketball games today.*

2. 老师要我们看这本书，而且还要看**三遍**。Lǎoshī yào wǒmen kàn zhè běn shū, érqiě hái yào kàn **sān biàn.**

TRANSLATION: *The teacher asked us to read this book three times.*

3. 说再见的时候妈妈在女儿的小脸上亲了**一口**。Shuō zàijiàn de shíhou māma zài nǚ'ér de xiǎo liǎn shàng qīn le **yì kǒu.**

TRANSLATION: *When saying goodbye, the mother gave her daughter a little kiss on the cheek.*

4. 哥哥经常去中国，已经去了**五次**。Gēge jīngcháng qù Zhōngguó, yǐjīng qù le **wǔ cì.**

TRANSLATION: *My older brother often goes to China. He has been there five times.*

5. 我们不知道怎么走了。你去问**一下**。Wǒmen bù zhīdào zěnme zǒu le. Nǐ qù wèn **yí xià.**

TRANSLATION: *We don't know how to get there. Go and ask quickly.*

6. 她只看了**一眼**，就知道那不是她的书包。Tā zhǐ kàn le **yì yǎn**, jiù zhīdào nà bú shì tā de shūbāo.

TRANSLATION: *She only took one glance and knew it was not her schoolbag.*

7. 要想知道肉里面做好了没有，切**一刀**一看就知道了。Yào xiǎng zhīdào ròu lǐmiàn zuò hǎo le méi yǒu, qiē **yì dāo** yí kàn jiù zhīdào le.

TRANSLATION: *If you want to know whether the meat is cooked inside, just cut it a little and you will know.*

8. 要想记住汉字怎么写，每个字要写**十遍**。Yào xiǎng jìzhù hànzì zěnme xiě, měi ge zì yào xiě **shí biàn.**

TRANSLATION: *If you want to remember how to write Chinese characters, you should write each character ten times.*

9. 她要和朋友一起去听**一场**音乐会。 Tā yào hé péngyou yìqǐ qù tīng **yì chǎng** yīnyuèhuì.

TRANSLATION: *She is going to listen to a concert with her friends.*

34. 金婚和银婚 Jīnhūn hé yínhūn
NUMBER FOCUS

1. 结婚五十年是金婚。 **Jiéhūn wǔshí nián shì jīn hūn.**

2. 结婚十三年是花边婚。 **Jiéhūn shísān nián shì huābiān hūn.**

3. 结婚三十年是珍珠婚。 **Jiéhūn sānshí nián shì zhēnzhū hūn.**

4. 结婚四年是花果婚。 **Jiéhūn sì nián shì huāguǒ hūn.**

5. 结婚一年是纸婚。 **Jiéhūn yì nián shì zhǐ hūn.**

6. 结婚六十年是钻石婚。 **Jiéhūn liùshí nián shì zuànshí hūn.**

7. 结婚二十年是瓷婚。 **Jiéhūn èrshí nián shì cí hūn.**

35. 饿了吗？È le ma?
TASTE BUD TANTALISER

1. They are in a restaurant.
2. Wang Peng was not hungry at first, but now he is hungry.
3. To see Wang Peng off and treat him to a farewell meal.
4. Chicken.
5. Corn cake.
6. They didn't order any drinks.

36. 翻译挑战 4 Fānyì tiǎozhàn 4
TRANSLATION CHALLENGE

1. 你做什么工作? **Nǐ zuò shénme gōngzuò?**

2. 你在哪里打网球? **Nǐ zài nǎlǐ dǎ wǎngqiú?**

EXPLANATION:

- Note that in informal situations, 哪儿 **nǎer** is an alternative to 哪里 **nǎlǐ**.

3. 你每天几点去上班 / 工作 / 打工? **Nǐ měitiān jǐdiǎn qù shàngbān / gōngzuò / dǎgōng?**

or

你每天什么时候去上班 / 工作 / 打工? **Nǐ měitiān shénme shíhou qù shàngbān / gōngzuò / dǎgōng?**

EXPLANATION:

- Instead of 每天 **měitiān**, you can also use 天天 **tiāntiān** to translate *every day*.

- 去上班 **qù shàngbān**, 去工作 **qù gōngzuò** and 去打工 **qù dǎgōng** can all be used to translate *go to work*, but 打工 **dǎgōng** tends to be used for hourly-paid, part-time jobs.

4. 谁帮(助)你学(习)中文/汉语? **Shéi bāng(zhù) nǐ xué(xí) Zhōngwén / Hànyǔ?**

EXPLANATION:

- Both 帮 **bāng** and 帮助 **bāngzhù** are correct, but 帮 **bāng** is more informal.

- Similarly, 学 **xué** is a less formal way of saying 学习 **xuéxí**.

- 中文 **Zhōngwén** refers to both written and spoken Chinese, while 汉语 **Hànyǔ** mainly refers to spoken Chinese.

5. 你更喜欢哪(一)本书？ **Nǐ gèng xǐhuan nǎ běn shū?**

EXPLANATION:

- Remember that the measure word used for a book is 本 **běn**.

6. 你有几条 / 多少条狗？ **Nǐ yǒu jǐ tiáo / duōshǎo tiáo gǒu?**
   or
   你有几只/多少只狗？ **Nǐ yǒu jǐ zhī / duōshǎo zhī gǒu?**

EXPLANATION:

- When you suspect the answer is fewer than ten, use 几 **jǐ** plus a measure word to ask *how many*?
- When you think the answer will be more than ten, use 多少 **duōshǎo** instead.
- With uncountable nouns like *air* or *water*, we use 多少 **duōshǎo** to ask *how much?* The measure word to use for dogs is either 条 **tiáo** or 只 **zhī**.

37. 聂华苓 Niè Huálíng
FAMOUS CHINESE SPEAKERS

1. Hualing Nieh Engle was born in 1925 and died in 2024.
2. The International Writing Program.
3. 1,400 writers from 150 countries.
4. "Mother of World Literature Organisation".
5. Her roots are in China and her branches are in Taiwan.
6. Her leaves are in Iowa and her fruits are all over the world.

38. 复合量词 Fùhé liàngcí
FOR GOOD MEASURE

EXERCISE 1 - MATCH

十人次 shí réncì — *10 people visiting / participating*

二十个架次 èrshí ge jiàcì — *20 flights*

五个船次 wǔ ge chuáncì — *5 ship journeys*

五十个车次 wǔshí ge chēcì — *50 bus journeys*

十个架次 shí ge jiàcì — *10 flights*

五个车次 wǔ ge chēcì — *5 bus journeys*

三十人次 sānshí réncì — *30 people visiting / participating*

二十个船次 èrshí ge chuáncì — *20 ship journeys*

一百个架次 yì bǎi ge jiàcì — *100 flights*

EXERCISE 2 - FILL IN THE GAPS

1. 这里的老师不是**个个**都很好。Zhèlǐ de lǎoshī bú shì **gègè** dōu hěn hǎo.

   TRANSLATION: *Not all of the teachers here are good.*

2. 上课了，学生**一个一个**走进了教室。Shàngkè le, xuésheng **yí ge yí ge** zǒujìn le jiàoshì.

   TRANSLATION: *The class started and the students walked into the classroom one by one.*

3. 这里的冬天天气很不好，**天天**都是阴天。Zhèlǐ de dōngtiān tiānqì hěn bù hǎo, **tiāntiān** dōu shì yīntiān.

   TRANSLATION: *The weather here in winter is very bad. It is cloudy every single day.*

4. 她写的书**本本**都是好书。 Tā xiě de shū **běnběn** dōu shì hǎo shū.

   TRANSLATION: *Each and every one of the books she wrote was good.*

5. 这么多书，我只能**一本一本**地看。 Zhème duō shū, wǒ zhǐnéng **yì běn yì běn** de kàn.

   TRANSLATION: *There are so many books. I can only read them one at a time.*

6. 日子**一天一天**过去了，她的身体慢慢好起来了。 Rìzi **yì tiān yì tiān** guòqù le, tā de shēntǐ mànmàn hǎo qǐlái le.

   TRANSLATION: *One day after another passed and her health slowly improved.*

7. 她去中国去了很多次，**次次**都去北京。 Tā qù Zhōngguó qù le hěn duō cì, **cìcì** dōu qù Běijīng.

   TRANSLATION: *She has been to China many times. Each and every time, she goes to Beijing.*

8. 他是足球迷，只要有比赛，他**场场**都要看。 Tā shì zúqiúmí, zhǐyào yǒu bǐsài, tā **chǎngchǎng** dōu yào kàn.

   TRANSLATION: *He is a football / soccer fan. He never misses a single game.*

9. 我们不要一起说话，要**一个一个**地讲话。 Wǒmen bú yào yìqǐ shuōhuà, yào **yí ge yí ge** de jiǎnghuà.

   TRANSLATION: *We should talk one person at a time.*

10. 哥哥**天天**都要喝咖啡，不喝咖啡就不能工作。 Gēge **tiāntiān** dōu yào hē kāfēi, bù hē kāfēi jiù bù néng gōngzuò.

    TRANSLATION: *My older brother needs to drink coffee every day. He can't work without it.*

39. 成千上万 Chéng qiān shàng wàn
NUMBER FOCUS

EXERCISE 1 - TRANSLATE

1. endless words to say, having a lot to say
2. an unstoppable force, with great momentum
3. a long and arduous journey, through countless hardships
4. a magnificent and varied scene, a grand spectacle
5. every word is priceless, words of huge value

EXERCISE 2 - FILL IN THE GAPS

1. 从北京出发, 他们走了很多天, 走过了**万水千山**, 最后才走到南京。 Cóng Běijīng chūfā, tāmen zǒu le hěn duō tiān, zǒu guò le **wàn shuǐ qiān shān**, zuìhòu cái zǒu dào Nánjīng.

   TRANSLATION: *Starting from Beijing, they walked for many days, crossed many rivers and climbed many mountains. Finally, they reached Nanjing.*

2. 你帮了我一个大忙, 我有**千言万语**, 可是只能说一句"谢谢你"。 Nǐ bāng le wǒ yí ge dà máng, wǒ yǒu **qiān yán wàn yǔ**, kěshì zhǐ néng shuō yí jù "xièxie nǐ".

   TRANSLATION: *You did me a big favour. I have so much to say, but all I can say is "thank you".*

3. 你的书不在我这里, **千真万确**。 不信你可以自己找一找。 Nǐ de shū bú zài wǒ zhèlǐ, **qiān zhēn wàn què**. Bú xìn nǐ kěyǐ zìjǐ zhǎo yì zhǎo.

   TRANSLATION: *Your book is not here with me. That is absolutely certain. If you don't believe me, you can see for yourself.*

4. 体育场里有很多人，**成千上万**的人在一起喊，"加油！"
   Tǐyùchǎng lǐ yǒu hěn duō rén, **chéng qiān shàng wàn** de rén zài yìqǐ hǎn, "jiāyóu!"
   TRANSLATION: *The stadium is full of people, with thousands upon thousands shouting together, "come on!"*

5. 这个运动员非常非常厉害，是我们**万里挑一**选出来的。 Zhè ge yùndòngyuán fēicháng fēicháng lìhai, shì wǒmen **wàn lǐ tiāo yī** xuǎn chūlái de.
   TRANSLATION: *This athlete is really very special. He's one in a million.*

40. 面条 Miàntiáo
TASTE BUD TANTALISER

1. 长命百岁! **Cháng mìng bǎi suì!**
2. You add the water into the flour.
3. Dry flour.
4. Fold it.
5. 15 minutes.

15-MINUTE COFFEE BREAKS

CHECKLIST
15-MINUTE COFFEE BREAKS

Reading Focus

Grammar Focus

Vocabulary Consolidation

41

乒乓球
Pīngpāngqiú
READING FOCUS

In this activity, we're focusing on a reading text about a sport that is well known across the world: 乒乓球 **pīngpāngqiú**. Table tennis was invented in England in 1900 and today it is popular internationally, especially in China. Read the text and answer the comprehension and language questions that follow to test your understanding. You'll encounter some vocabulary specific to table tennis in the text, so you may need to use the vocabulary list to help you.

* * *

Pīng	pāng	qiú,	yǒu	xiē	xiàng	wǎng	qiú,	shì	yì	zhǒng	shì	jiè
乒	乓	球,	有	些	像	网	球,	是	一	种	世	界

liú	xíng	de	yùn	dòng.	Bǐ	sài	yǒu	tuán	tǐ,	dān	dǎ,	shuāng
流	行	的	运	动。	比	赛	有	团	体、	单	打、	双

dǎ	děng	děng.	Pīng	pāng	qiú	bǐ	sài	shì	11	fēn	yì	jú,
打	等	等。	乒	乓	球	比	赛	是	11	分	一	局,

cháng cháng shì wǔ jú sān shèng huò zhě qī jú sì shèng.
常 常 是 五 局 三 胜 或 者 七 局 四 胜。

Bǐ sài de shí hou, shuāng fāng gé zhe liǎng ge zhuō zi
比 赛 的 时 候, 双 方 隔 着 两 个 桌 子

duì dǎ, zhí dào yì fāng wú fǎ huí qiú, huò zhě dǎ
对 打, 直 到 一 方 无 法 回 球, 或 者 打

de qiú méi yǒu luò zài duì fāng de zhuō zi shàng, duì
的 球 没 有 落 在 对 方 的 桌 子 上, 对

fāng jiù dé yì fēn. Fā qiú shí, yì fāng xiān fā liǎng
方 就 得 一 分。 发 球 时, 一 方 先 发 两

ge qiú, rán hòu lìng wài yì fāng zài fā liǎng ge qiú,
个 球, 然 后 另 外 一 方 再 发 两 个 球,

yì zhí lún huàn xià qù. Xiān dé 11 fēn de rén huò
一 直 轮 换 下 去。 先 得 11 分 的 人 获

shèng. Dàn shì rú guǒ liǎng ge rén dōu dé le 10 fēn,
胜。 但 是 如 果 两 个 人 都 得 了 10 分,

nà jiù yào jì xù dǎ xià qù, xiān dé liǎng fēn de
那 就 要 继 续 打 下 去, 先 得 两 分 的

rén huò shèng. Nǐ yào bú yào lái dǎ yì jú?
人 获 胜。 你 要 不 要 来 打 一 局?

VOCABULARY

乒乓球 **pīngpāngqiú**   *table tennis, ping-pong*
网球 **wǎngqiú**   *tennis*
团体 **tuántǐ**   *team event*
单打 **dāndǎ**   *singles event*

双打 shuāngdǎ	*doubles event*
局 jú	*game*
五局三胜 wǔ jú sān shèng	*best of five (games)*
七局四胜 qī jú sì shèng	*best of seven (games)*
隔着 gézhe	*across*
发球 fāqiú	*to serve*
双方 shuāngfāng	*both sides*
得一分 dé yì fēn	*to win one point*
获胜 huòshèng	*to win*

EXERCISE 1 - COMPREHENSION

Answer the following questions in English.

1. Can table tennis be played in doubles?

   ✎_____

   _____

2. How many points are there in one game?

   ✎_____

   _____

3. How is a point scored in a table tennis match?

   ✎_____

   _____

4. What information does the text give about serving?

   ✎_____

   _____

5. When the two players tie, how do they decide who wins?

✎_____

_____

EXERCISE 2 - TRANSLATE

Translate the following words or phrases from the text into English.

1. 网球

✎_____

2. 运动

✎_____

3. 团体

✎_____

4. 轮换

✎_____

5. 获胜

✎_____

EXERCISE 3 - FIND THE CHINESE

Find the Chinese in the text for the following words or phrases.

1. to serve

✎_____

2. singles competition

✎_____

3. best of five

✎_____

4. win a point

✎_____

5. play a game

✎_____

* * *

太棒了！ **Tài bàng le!** When you're happy with your answers, you can check them on pages 242-243.

42

怎么用"的、地、得"
Zěnme yòng "dè, dì, dé"
GRAMMAR FOCUS

In this grammar activity, we are looking at 的 dè, 地 dì and 得 dé, the three most frequently used particles in Chinese. These particles are easily confused, but they are used very differently from each other. Read the explanation below, then have a go at the exercise that follows to test your understanding. 加油! Jiāyóu!

* * *

的、地、得 de

First of all, a note on pronunciation: although the characters 的 dè, 地 dì and 得 dé are pronounced differently from one another in certain contexts, when they are used as particles in the contexts we're about to see, 的, 地 and 得 are all pronounced as a neutral tone **de** within sentences.

的

Let's look at how 的 is used in the following phrases:

A. **mèimei de gōngyù**
妹妹的公寓   *my younger sister's apartment*

B. **piàoliang de yīfu**
漂亮的衣服   *beautiful clothes*

C. **shūshu zuò de fàn**
叔叔做的饭   *the food that uncle cooked*

In phrase A 的 is between two nouns. It is indicating possession (the apartment belongs to the sister).

Phrase B has 的 between an adjective and a noun. The adjective is modifying the noun (describing it as *beautiful*).

In phrase C 的 is between a verb phrase and a noun. The verb phrase is serving as an attributive to modify the noun (describing it as the food that uncle cooked).

All three phrases have a noun after 的.

Now, let's see these phrases in full sentences to understand them further.

A. **Mèimei de gōngyù zài shìzhōngxīn.**
妹妹的公寓在市中心。

My younger sister's apartment is in the city centre.

B. **Piàoliang de yīfu dōu hěn guì.**
漂亮的衣服都很贵。

Beautiful clothes are always very expensive.

C. **Shūshu zuò de fàn zuì hǎochī.**
叔叔做的饭最好吃。

The food that uncle cooks is always the best.

地

Now let's turn our attention to 地.

Pay attention to how this particle is used in the following sentences:

A. **Tā hěn kuài de zǒu le.**
他很快地走了。

He quickly left.

B. **Qǐng mànmàn de shuō.**
请慢慢地说。

Please speak slowly.

C. **Wǒmen qù nàlǐ hǎohāor de wán liǎng tiān.**
我们去那里好好儿地玩两天。

Let's go there and have fun for two days.

As you can see from the three examples, an *adverb* + 地 + a *verb* is used to describe how an action is carried out (for example, speaking *slowly* or leaving *quickly*).

得

Finally, let's look at how 得 is used:

A. **Tā shuō Zhōngwén shuō de hěn màn, kěshì shuō Yīngwén shuō de hěn kuài.**
他说中文说得很慢，可是说英文说得很快。
He speaks Chinese very slowly, but he speaks English very fast.

B. **Wǒ zuówǎn shuìjiào shuì de hěn bù hǎo.**
我昨晚睡觉睡得很不好。
I slept very badly last night.

C. **Shōudào kǎoshì de jiéguǒ, yǒude rén gāoxìng de tiào le qǐlái,
yǒude rén shāngxīn de kū le qǐlái.**

收到考试的结果，有的人高兴得跳了起来，有的人
伤心得哭了起来。

*On receiving the exam results, some people were so happy that they were
jumping for joy, while others were so sad that they started crying.*

As you can see, 得 follows a verb or an adjective. When it follows
a verb, it carries a descriptive complement after it showing, for
example, that the subject can do something fast or slowly, well or
not well. When 得 follows an adjective, it carries a verb after it. It
means the subject is so happy or sad (for example) that they have to
do something.

A SUMMARY OF 的、地、得

attributive + 的 + *noun*

adverb + 地 + *verb*

verb + 得 + *adjective*

or

adjective + 得 + *verb*

EXERCISE

Let's fill in the blanks with 的, 地 or 得, according to the context.

1. 妹妹 ✎_____ 书包很小。 **Mèimei de shūbāo hěn
xiǎo.**

2. 她很快 ✎_____ 就把书还给了我。 **Tā hěn kuài
de jiù bǎ shū huángěi le wǒ.**

3. 姐姐写英文写 ✎_____ 很快，可是写汉字写
   ✎_____ 很慢。 Jiějie xiě Yīngwén xiě de hěn kuài,
   kěshì xiě Hànzì xiě de hěn màn.

4. 我累 ✎_____ 站不起来了。Wǒ lèi de zhàn bù qǐlái le.

5. 妈妈给我做 ✎_____ 衣服总是太大。 Māma gěi
   wǒ zuò de yīfu zǒngshì tài dà.

6. 最好 ✎_____ 大学不一定最贵。 Zuìhǎo de dàxué
   bù yídìng zuì guì.

7. 你拉什么乐器拉 ✎_____ 最好? Nǐ lā shénme yuèqì lā
   de zuìhǎo?

8. 弟弟慢慢 ✎_____ 拿出来了他的手机。 Dìdi
   mànmàn de ná chūlái le tā de shǒujī.

9. 我在这里吃 ✎_____ 很好，玩 ✎_____ 也很好。
   Wǒ zài zhèlǐ chī de hěn hǎo, wán de yě hěn hǎo.

10. 姐姐忙 ✎_____ 没有时间吃饭。 Jiějie máng de méi
    yǒu shíjiān chīfàn.

* * *

Once you're happy with your choices, turn to pages 243-244 to check
the answers.

43

旅行
Lǚxíng
VOCABULARY CONSOLIDATION

In this activity, we're going to practise some vocabulary on the topic of travel. We've chosen 20 words or phrases on this topic and have put together four exercises which will help you to familiarise yourself with this vocabulary. Make sure you've read through the list a few times, then cover it with your hand or a piece of paper and try to complete the exercises that follow without looking. 祝你成功! **Zhù nǐ chénggōng!**

* * *

旅行社 **lǚxíngshè**	*travel agency*
大使馆 **dàshǐguǎn**	*embassy*
申请签证 **shēnqǐng qiānzhèng**	*to apply for a visa*
到达 **dàodá**	*to arrive*
登机牌 **dēngjīpái**	*boarding pass*
时差 **shíchā**	*time difference*

出发 chūfā	*to set off*
观景 guānjǐng	*sightseeing*
迷路 mílù	*to be lost*
打行李 dǎ xíngli	*to pack a suitcase*
乘邮船 chéng yóuchuán	*to go on a cruise*
行程 xíngchéng	*itinerary*
住酒店 zhù jiǔdiàn	*to stay in a hotel*
旅游问讯处 lǚyóu wènxùnchù	*tourist information office*
度假 dùjià	*to go on holiday, to take a vacation*
护照 hùzhào	*passport*
地图 dìtú	*map*
照相 zhàoxiàng	*to take photos*
游客 yóukè	*tourist*
出差 chūchāi	*to go on a business trip*

EXERCISE 1 - TRANSLATE

Cover up the list above and translate the following words and phrases into Chinese.

1. itinerary

   ✎ _____

2. to go on holiday / vacation

   ✎ _____

3. travel agency

✎_____

4. to be lost

✎_____

5. to pack a suitcase

✎_____

EXERCISE 2 - WHAT'S MISSING?

1. Take another look at the five words and phrases in the following list:

旅行社
大使馆
申请签证
到达
登机牌

Now, cover up the list above with your hand or a piece of paper and complete the list below with the one that's missing.

登机牌
申请签证
大使馆
旅行社

✎_____

2. Let's do the same with another five words or phrases from the list:

时差
出发
迷路
观景
打行李

Now, cover them up and spot what's missing from the list below:

出发
迷路
时差
打行李

✎_____

3. Here are the next five:

乘邮船
行程
住酒店
旅游问讯处
度假

Which one is missing from the following list?

行程
住酒店
旅游问讯处
度假

✎_____

4. Here is the final list of five pieces of vocabulary:

护照
地图
照相
游客
出差

Cover them up and fill in the gap with the missing word or phrase.

地图
照相
护照
游客

✎_____

EXERCISE 3 - ODD ONE OUT

1. Which *two* of the words or phrases from the list below would you be unlikely to use when talking about travelling for work?

乘邮船
行程
住酒店
旅游问讯处
护照

✎_____

✎_____

2. Which *three* of the following words or phrases would you be unlikely to use when talking with some friends from Shanghai about doing a road trip around China?

时差
行程
住酒店
大使馆
护照

✎_____

✎_____

✎_____

EXERCISE 4 - FILL IN THE GAPS
Fill in each gap with the most appropriate word or phrase from the list. If you need to, you can refer back to the vocabulary list to help you.

1. 去一个国家旅游之前, 要先去那个国家的大使馆
   ✎_____。 **Qù yí ge guójiā lǚyóu zhīqián, yào xiān qù nà ge guójiā de dàshǐguǎn**
   ✎_____ .

2. 北京和纽约的 ✎_____ 是几个
   小时? **Běijīng hé Niǔyuē de** ✎_____
   shì jǐ ge xiǎoshí?

3. 出去旅行, 我喜欢 ✎_____,
   不喜欢住在朋友家里。 **Chūqù lǚxíng, wǒ xǐhuan**
   ✎_____ **, bù xǐhuan zhù zài**
   péngyou jiālǐ.

4. 上飞机的时候，一定要出示

✎_____ 。 **Shàng fēijī de shíhou,**
yídìng yào chūshì ✎_____ .

5. 应该离开酒店出发了，可是我还没有

✎_____ 。 **Yīnggāi líkāi jiǔdiàn**
chūfā le, kěshì wǒ hái méi yǒu

✎_____ .

* * *

When you're ready, turn to pages 244-246 to find the answers to the
exercises.

44

我的朋友李萌
Wǒ de péngyou Lǐ Méng
READING FOCUS

In this reading activity, we are going to read a paragraph which will help you practise useful, everyday language that you can use to describe a person. Use the vocabulary list and the pinyin as required to help you as you read. Then, answer the comprehension questions and try writing your own paragraph giving a description of a person.

* * *

Lǐ	Méng	shì	wǒ	de	hǎo	péng	you,	wǒ	men	zài	yí
李	萌	是	我	的	好	朋	友,	我	们	在	一

ge	gōng	sī	gōng	zuò.	Wǒ	men	dōu	shì	gōng	chéng	shī.
个	公	司	工	作。	我	们	都	是	工	程	师。

Tā	shì	cóng	Zhōng	guó	lái	de.	Tā	jīn	nián	èr	shí
她	是	从	中	国	来	的。	她	今	年	二	十

bā	suì.	Tā	wǔ	chǐ	shí	yī	cùn	gāo.	Tā	de	tóu
八	岁。	她	五	尺	十	一	寸	高。	她	的	头

203

发是黑色的，眼睛是褐色的。她
特别喜欢笑，还常常讲笑话。她
上衣喜欢穿西装，裤子喜欢穿
牛仔裤。她喜欢吃蔬菜和水果。
她不喜欢吃肉，但是他喜欢吃
鱼和虾。她经常自己做饭。她做
饭做得很好，有时候还请我去
她家吃饭。有空的时候，我们喜
欢打乒乓球和游泳。我们还常
常一起去听音乐会，也常常出
去旅游。我们一起去过亚洲、非
洲和南美洲。

VOCABULARY

她......高 tā ... gāo	*her height is ...*
黑色 hēi sè	*black*
褐色 hè sè	*brown*
特别 tè bié	*especially*
做饭做得很好 zuòfàn zuò de hěn hǎo	*good at cooking*
有空的时候 yǒukòng de shíhou	*during her free time*
乒乓球 pīngpāngqiú	*table tennis*
亚洲 Yà zhōu	*Asia*
非洲 Fēi zhōu	*Africa*
南美洲 Nán měi zhōu	*South America*

EXERCISE 1 - COMPREHENSION

Answer the following questions in English.

1. What does Li Meng do for a living?

   ✎_____

   _____

2. What colour is her hair?

   ✎_____

   _____

3. What does she like to wear?

✎_____

_____

4. What does she like to eat? What doesn't she like to eat?

✎_____

_____

5. What sports does she play?

✎_____

_____

6. Where has she been travelling?

✎_____

_____

EXERCISE 2 - OVER TO YOU

Now it's your turn! Use phrases from the text and the vocabulary list to help you write a short paragraph like the one about 李萌 **Lǐ Méng**. It can be about anyone you like: for example a friend, a family member, a colleague or an imaginary person. Write in Chinese characters or in pinyin – whatever is most useful for your learning.

✎_____

_____

_____

_____

_____

_____

_____

_____

_____

_____

_____

_____

_____

_____

_____

_____

_____

_____

_____

* * *

When you're ready, turn to page 246 to read the answers to Exercise 1.

45

比较
Bǐjiào
GRAMMAR FOCUS

In this grammar activity, we are looking at how to make comparisons between two things in Chinese. Read the explanation below, then have a go at the two exercises that follow. 加油! **Jiāyóu!**

* * *

POSITIVE COMPARISONS

Look at the example below. It creates a comparison between two people using the structure:

subject 1 (the brother) + 比 **bǐ** + *subject 2* (the sister) + *adjective*

Dìdi bǐ mèimei gāo.
弟弟比妹妹高。
My younger brother is taller than my younger sister.

The next sentence goes one step further to give the height difference.

Dìdi bǐ mèimei gāo liǎngcùn.

弟弟比妹妹高两寸。

My younger brother is two inches taller than my younger sister.

NEGATIVE COMPARISONS

Now let's see how to form negative comparisons. In reality, negative comparisons may tend to be used less than positive comparisons, as people naturally rephrase them into positive comparisons, just as we often do in English. However, it's still important to know how to form them.

Mèimei méi yǒu dìdi gāo.

妹妹没有弟弟高。

My younger sister is not as tall as my younger brother.

Notice that we can use 没有 **méi yǒu** to express negative comparisons. Alternatively, we can use 不如 **bùrú**, as you'll see in the next example.

Mèimei bùrú dìdi gāo.

妹妹不如弟弟高。

My younger sister is not as tall as my younger brother.

Both the sentence with 没有 **méi yǒu** and the sentence with 不如 **bùrú** mean exactly the same.

MORE EXAMPLES

Let's look at some more sentences with comparisons.

Zhè běn shū bǐ nà běn shū guì sānshí měiyuán.

这本书比那本书贵三十美元。

This book is $30 more expensive than that book.

Wǒ méi yǒu nǐ nàme máng.

我没有你那么忙。

I'm not as busy as you are.

Jīntiān de tiānqì bǐ zuótiān hǎo hěn duō.

今天的天气比昨天好很多。

Today's weather is much better than yesterday's.

Wǒ kànshū bùrú nǐ kànshū kàn de kuài.

我看书不如你看书看得快。

I don't read books as quickly as you do.

Nǐ bǐ wǒ pǎo de kuài, kěshì nǐ méi yǒu wǒ tiào de gāo.

你比我跑得快，可是你没有我跳得高。

You run faster than me, but you don't jump as high as I do.

EXERCISE 1 - CREATE COMPARISONS

Rewrite the following sentences to create comparative sentences with 比 **bǐ**. We've done the first one for you.

这本书很有意思，可是那本书不那么有意思。**Zhè běn shū hěn yǒuyìsi, kěshì nà běn shū bù nàme yǒuyìsi.** ⎯⎯⎯→ 这本书比那本书有意思。**Zhè běn shū bǐ nà běn shū yǒuyìsi.**

1. 我的裙子三十美元，你的裙子二十美元。**Wǒ de qúnzi sānshí měiyuán, nǐ de qúnzi èrshí měiyuán.**

✎ _____

_____

2. 妹妹跑得很快，姐姐跑得不那么快。 **Mèimei pǎo de hěn kuài, jiějie pǎo de bú nàme kuài.**

✎ _____

_____

3. 麦克身高六尺，李明身高五尺。 **Màikè shēngāo liù chǐ, Lǐ Míng shēngāo wǔ chǐ.**

✎ _____

_____

4. 我写英文写得很漂亮，可是写汉字写得不那么漂亮。 **Wǒ xiě Yīngwén xiě de hěn piàoliang, kěshì xiě Hànzì xiě de bú nàme piàoliang.**

✎ _____

_____

EXERCISE 2 - Q&A

Write an answer to each of the questions using one of the comparative structures we've learned. Base the answer on the English statement provided, writing in characters or in pinyin.

1. Q: 你爸爸和你妈妈谁高？ **Nǐ bàba hé nǐ māma shéi gāo?**

A: ✎ _____

_____

My father is three inches taller than my mother.

2. Q: 妈妈做饭做得好吃还是爸爸做饭做得好吃？
   Māma zuòfàn zuò de hǎochī háishi bàba zuòfàn zuò de hǎochī?

   A: ✎_____

   _____

   My mother cooks much better than my father.

3. Q: 你跳舞跳得好还是你妹妹跳舞跳得好？ **Nǐ tiàowǔ tiào de hǎo háishì nǐ mèimei tiàowǔ tiào de hǎo?**

   A: ✎_____

   _____

   I don't dance as well as my sister.

4. Q: 英语比汉语难学吗？ **Yīngyǔ bǐ Hànyǔ nán xué ma?**

   A: ✎_____

   _____

   No, English is not as difficult to learn as Chinese.

5. Q: 明天的天气比今天的天气好吗？ **Míngtiān de tiānqì bǐ jīntiān de tiānqì hǎo ma?**

   A: ✎_____

   _____

   The weather tomorrow will not be as good as today's weather.

* * *

Once you've finished the exercises, turn to pages 247-248 to check your answers.

46

音乐
Yīnyuè
VOCABULARY CONSOLIDATION

In this activity, we're going to practise some vocabulary on the topic of music. We have chosen 20 words and phrases on this topic and you have three exercises to help you familiarise yourself with the vocabulary. Make sure you've read through the list a few times, then cover it with your hand or a piece of paper and try to complete the exercises that follow without looking. 祝你成功! **Zhù nǐ chénggōng!**

* * *

Pay attention to the verb used with each musical instrument in the list, which refers to the way in which the instrument is played. The vocabulary is divided into five categories and a specific verb is used for each category.

The first four instruments are used with the verb 吹 **chuī**, which means *to blow*.

吹法国号 **chuī fǎguóhào**		*to play the French horn*
吹唢呐 **chuī suǒnà**		*to play suona (a type of Chinese horn)*
吹口琴 **chuī kǒuqín**		*to play the harmonica*
吹笛子 **chuī dízi**		*to play the flute*

The next four instruments are used with the verb 拉 **lā**, which means *to pull* or *to drag*, and refers to the way the bow is drawn across the strings of a string instrument.

拉小提琴 **lā xiǎotíqín**	*to play the violin*
拉大提琴 **lā dàtíqín**	*to play the cello*
拉中提琴 **lā zhōngtíqín**	*to play the viola*
拉二胡 **lā èrhú**	*to play erhu (a type of Chinese violin with two strings)*

The verb 弹 **tán** literally means *to spring* or *to pluck* and is used with keyboard or plucked instruments.

弹钢琴 **tán gāngqín**	*to play the piano*
弹吉他 **tán jítā**	*to play the guitar*
弹琵琶 **tán pípá**	*to play pipa (a type of Chinese guitar)*
弹电子琴 **tán diànzǐqín**	*to play the keyboard*

Next, 打 **dǎ** means *to hit* or *to strike*, and so is used to talk about playing percussion instruments.

打鼓 **dǎgǔ**	*to play the drums*
打锣 **dǎluó**	*to play the gong*
打镲 **dǎchǎ**	*to play the cymbals*
打铃 **dǎlíng**	*to play the bells*

The final four pieces of vocabulary are about singing and so use the verb 唱 **chàng.**

唱歌 **chànggē**	*to sing (songs)*
唱民歌 **chàng míngē**	*to sing folk songs*
唱歌剧 **chàng gējù**	*to sing opera*
唱京剧 **chàng jīngjù**	*to sing Beijing opera*

EXERCISE 1 - TRANSLATE

Translate the following words and phrases into Chinese. Try not to refer to the vocabulary list.

1. to sing songs

   ✎ _____

2. to play the violin

   ✎ _____

3. to play the French horn

   ✎ _____

4. to play the piano

   ✎ _____

5. to play the bells

   ✎ _____

EXERCISE 2 - WHAT'S MISSING?

1. Take another look at the five words and phrases in the following list:

吹法国号
拉小提琴
弹钢琴
打鼓
唱歌

Now, cover up the list above with your hand or a piece of paper and complete the following list with the one that's missing.

唱歌
吹法国号
打鼓
弹钢琴

✎_____

2. Let's do the same with another five words or phrases from the list:

吹唢呐
拉大提琴
弹吉他
打锣
唱民歌

Now, cover them up and spot what's missing from the list below:

唱民歌
吹唢呐
拉大提琴
弹吉他

✎_____

3. Here are the next five:

吹口琴

拉中提琴

弹琵琶

打镲

唱歌剧

Which one is missing from the following list?

唱歌剧

拉中提琴

吹口琴

打镲

✎_____

4. Here is the final list of five pieces of vocabulary:

吹笛子

拉二胡

弹电子琴

打铃

唱京剧

Cover them and fill in the missing word or phrase.

打铃

拉二胡

吹笛子

弹电子琴

✎_____

EXERCISE 3 - FILL IN THE GAPS

Fill in each gap with an appropriate word from the list. If you need to, you can refer back to the vocabulary list to help you. We've also added some extra vocabulary below to help you. Note that there is more than one correct answer for each sentence.

1. 她的爸爸喜欢管乐*, 他会

   ✏_____ 。

   Tā de bàba xǐhuan guǎn lè, tā huì

   ✏_____ .

2. 她的妈妈喜欢弦乐, 她会

   ✏_____ 。

   Tā de māma xǐhuan xiányuè, tā huì

   ✏_____ .

3. 她的姐姐喜欢弹拨乐, 她会

   ✏_____ 。

   Tā de jiějie xǐhuan tánbōyuè, tā huì

   ✏_____ .

4. 她的哥哥喜欢打击乐, 他会

   ✏_____ 。

   Tā de gēge xǐhuan dǎjī yuè, tā huì

   ✏_____ .

5. 她很喜欢唱歌, 还会

   ✏_____ 。

   Tā hěn xǐhuan chànggē, hái huì

   ✏_____ .

*Here is some extra vocabulary to help you if you need it:

管乐 **guǎnyuè**	*wind instruments (e.g. French horn, flute)*
弦乐 **xiányuè**	*string instruments (e.g. violin, cello)*
弹拨乐 **tánbōyuè**	*keyboard and plucked instruments (e.g. piano, guitar)*
打击乐 **dǎjīyuè**	*percussion instruments (e.g. drums, bells)*

* * *

When you're happy with your answers, turn to pages 248-249 to check them.

47

中国城
Zhōngguóchéng
READING FOCUS

In this activity, we are going to work on a text about 中国城
zhōngguóchéng, *Chinatown*. Try reading the text with the help of
the vocabulary list, then answer the comprehension questions in
Chinese to test your understanding and your writing skills.

* * *

Yǒu	rén	shuō,	yǒu	rén	de	dì	fāng	jiù	yǒu	Zhōng	guó
有	人	说，	有	人	的	地	方	就	有	中	国

rén,	yǒu	Zhōng	guó	rén	de	dì	fāng	jiù	yǒu	zhōng	guó
人，	有	中	国	人	的	地	方	就	有	中	国

chéng.	Dà	gài	zhēn	de	shì	zhè	yàng.	Shì	jiè	shàng	de
城。	大	概	真	的	是	这	样。	世	界	上	的

hěn	duō	chéng	shì	dōu	yǒu	dà	dà	xiǎo	xiǎo	de	zhōng
很	多	城	市	都	有	大	大	小	小	的	中

国城。中国城一般都不在这个

城市的最中心，但是离市中心

又不会太远。中国城不是一个

有城墙的城堡，而是华人商店、

中餐馆、中药店、各类会馆、中文

学校集中的几条大街。比较大

的中国城都有一个牌楼，上面

写着四个大字，"天下为公"。每到

过春节的时候，中国城都会举

行游行，有各种花车，当然也有

舞龙的队伍，舞狮子的队伍。这

时候很多华人和当地的老百

姓都会来观看，很多人都会跟

221

nǐ shuō, "Gōng xǐ fā cái!" Zhè shí nǐ yě yào huí
你 说, "恭喜 发 财!" 这 时 你 也 要 回

fù rén jiā shuō "Gōng xǐ fā cái!"
复 人 家 说 "恭喜 发 财!"

VOCABULARY

世界上 shìjiè shàng	*in the world*
大大小小的 dà dà xiǎo xiǎo de	*big or small*
不是......而是...... bùshì ... érshì ...	*it is not ... but ...*
城墙 chéngqiáng	*city wall*
城堡 chéngbǎo	*castle*
中餐馆 zhōngcānguǎn	*Chinese restaurant*
中药店 zhōngyàodiàn	*Chinese medicine store*
各类 gèlèi	*all kinds of*
会馆 huìguǎn	*association*
集中 jízhōng	*concentrated*
牌楼 páilou	*archway, gateway*
天下为公 tiānxià wéi gōng	*all people are for others, the world is one community*
过春节 guò Chūnjié	*to celebrate the Chinese New Year*
举行 jǔxíng	*to hold*
游行 yóuxíng	*parade*
花车 huāchē	*float*
舞龙 wǔlóng	*dragon dance*
舞狮 wǔshī	*lion dance*

观看 guānkàn   *spectate*

恭喜发财 Gōngxǐ fācái!   *May you be prosperous!*

回复 huífù   *to reply*

EXERCISE - COMPREHENSION AND WRITING

Write your answers to the following comprehension questions either in Chinese characters or in pinyin.

1. 有人说，有人的地方就会有什么？Yǒurén shuō, yǒurén de dìfāng jiù huì yǒu shénme?

   _____

   _____

   _____

2. 根据短文，世界上的城市一般都有中国城吗？Gēnjù duǎn wén, shìjiè shàng de chéngshì yībān dōu yǒu zhōngguóchéng ma?

   _____

   _____

   _____

3. 中国城都是一样大吗？ **Zhōngguóchéng dōu shì yīyàng dà ma?**

_____

_____

_____

4. 中国城一般在不在市中心？ **Zhōngguóchéng yībān zài bùzài shìzhōngxīn?**

_____

_____

_____

5. 中国城是不是一个城堡？ **Zhōngguóchéng shìbùshì yī ge chéngbǎo?**

_____

_____

_____

6. 中国城都有什么？ **Zhōngguóchéng dōu yǒu shénme?**

_____

_____

_____

7. 过春节的时候华人做什么? **Guò Chūnjié de shíhòu huárén zuò shénme?**

✎_____

_____

_____

8. 如果别人对你说"恭喜发财",你应该说什么? **Rúguǒ biérén duì nǐ shuō "Gōngxǐ fācái", nǐ yīnggāi shuō shénme?**

✎_____

_____

_____

* * *

When you're ready, turn to pages 250-251 to see our suggested answers.

48

怎么用"被"
Zěnme yòng "bèi"
GRAMMAR FOCUS

In this grammar activity, we are looking at the passive marker 被 **bèi**. Read the explanation below to learn how to use 被 **bèi** in passive sentences, then have a go at the two exercises that follow. 加油! **Jiāyóu!**

* * *

THE PASSIVE VOICE

Passive sentences are sentences in which something *is done* rather than someone *doing something*. For example, *Mike took away an apple* is an active sentence, while *the apple was taken away (by Mike)* is a passive sentence.

FORMING PASSIVE SENTENCES USING 被 bèi

To understand how to use 被 **bèi** in Chinese, let's start by looking at the following active sentence:

Màikè názǒu le yí ge píngguǒ.
麦克拿走了一个苹果。
Mike took away an apple.

As you can see, this is the straightforward structure of *subject* (麦克) + *verb* (拿走了) + *object* (一个苹果).

The following example is a passive sentence, following the structure of *object* + 被 **bèi** + *agent* (the doer of the action) + *verb*.

Píngguǒ bèi Màikè názǒu le.
苹果被麦克拿走了。
The apple was taken away by Mike.

Both of these sentences tell us that Mike did something. However, the first sentence simply states that *Mike took away an apple*, while the second emphasises that the apple was taken by Mike and not by anyone else.

Look at the next sentence. This time, the doer of the action (known grammatically as the "agent") is omitted, but we still know it is a passive sentence.

Píngguǒ bèi názǒu le.
苹果被拿走了。
The apple was taken away.

MORE EXAMPLES

Let's look at some more examples with 被 **bèi**:

Wǒ jīngcháng bèi rènwéi shì Hánguórén.

我经常被认为是韩国人。

I am often mistaken for a Korean person.

Suǒyǒu fángjiān dōu bèi dǎsǎo le liǎng biàn, hěn gānjìng le.

所有房间都被打扫了两遍，很干净了。

All the rooms were cleaned twice. They are very clean now.

Now it's over to you to practise using 被 **bèi** in these two exercises.

EXERCISE 1 - TRANSFORM

Rewrite the following sentences to create passive sentences with 被 **bèi**. We've done the first one as an example.

爸爸吃了妈妈的水果。 **Bàba chī le māma de shuǐguǒ.** ⟶
妈妈的水果被爸爸吃了。 **Māma de shuǐguǒ bèi bàba chī le.**

1. 弟弟不小心打坏了电视。 **Dìdi bù xiǎoxīn dǎ huài le diànshì.**

   ✎_____

   _____

2. 妹妹整理好了我的房间。 **Mèimei zhěnglǐ hǎo le wǒ de fángjiān.**

   ✎_____

   _____

3. 有人偷走了我的书包。 **Yǒurén tōu zǒu le wǒ de shūbāo.**

✎＿＿＿＿＿＿＿＿＿＿＿＿＿＿＿＿＿＿＿＿＿＿＿＿

＿＿＿＿＿＿＿＿＿＿＿＿＿＿＿＿＿＿＿＿＿＿＿＿＿＿

4. 她的朋友请她去吃饭了。 **Tā de péngyou qǐng tā qù chīfàn le.**

✎＿＿＿＿＿＿＿＿＿＿＿＿＿＿＿＿＿＿＿＿＿＿＿＿

＿＿＿＿＿＿＿＿＿＿＿＿＿＿＿＿＿＿＿＿＿＿＿＿＿＿

EXERCISE 2 - Q&A

Write an answer to each of the questions based on the English statement provided. Use 被 **bèi** in each answer and write in characters or in pinyin.

1. Q. 我的书去哪里了？**Wǒ de shū qù nǎlǐ le?**

A. ✎＿＿＿＿＿＿＿＿＿＿＿＿＿＿＿＿＿＿＿＿＿＿

＿＿＿＿＿＿＿＿＿＿＿＿＿＿＿＿＿＿＿＿＿＿＿＿＿

Your book was taken away by your younger sister.

2. Q. 你买的新手机呢？**Nǐ mǎi de xīn shǒujī ne?**

A. ✎＿＿＿＿＿＿＿＿＿＿＿＿＿＿＿＿＿＿＿＿＿＿

＿＿＿＿＿＿＿＿＿＿＿＿＿＿＿＿＿＿＿＿＿＿＿＿＿

My new phone was stolen.

3. Q. 你今天怎么没有开车来上班？**Nǐ jīntiān zěnme méi yǒu kāichē lái shàngbān?**

   A. ✎ _____

   _____

   My car was driven away by my daughter.

4. Q. 这本书怎么样？**Zhè běn shū zěnmeyàng?**

   A. ✎ _____

   _____

   This book is very good. It has been translated into many languages.

5. Q. 你的那个同学为什么这么高兴？**Nǐ de nà ge tóngxué wèishénme zhè me gāoxìng?**

   A. ✎ _____

   _____

   She was praised by our teacher.

* * *

太棒了！**Tài bàng le!** When you're ready, you can check your answers on pages 251-252.

49

新科技
Xīn kējì
VOCABULARY CONSOLIDATION

In this activity, we're going to practise some vocabulary about new technology. We have chosen 20 words and phrases and have put together four exercises which will help you familiarise yourself with vocabulary to do with transportation, shopping, communication and artificial intelligence. Make sure you've read through the list a few times, then cover it with your hand or a piece of paper and try to complete the exercises that follow without looking. 祝你成功! **Zhù nǐ chénggōng!**

* * *

高铁 **gāotiě**   *high-speed train*
网约车 **wǎngyuēchē**   *taxi ordered online*
电动汽车 **diàndòng qìchē**   *electric car*
无人驾驶 **wúrén jiàshǐ**   *self-driven*
无人机 **wúrénjī**   *drone*

导航 dǎoháng	GPS, satellite navigation
网上购物 wǎngshàng gòuwù	online shopping
网上点餐 wǎngshàng diǎncān	to order food online
亚马逊 Yàmǎxùn	Amazon
快递 kuàidì	express delivery
支付宝 Zhīfùbǎo	Alipay
扫码 sǎomǎ	to scan a QR code
人工智能 réngōng zhìnéng	artificial intelligence
脑机对接 nǎojī duìjiē	brain-computer interface
人脸识别 rénliǎn shíbié	facial recognition
机器人 jīqìrén	robot
谷歌 Gǔgē	Google
脸书 Liǎnshū	Facebook
微信 Wēixìn	WeChat
短信 duǎnxìn	message

EXERCISE 1 - TRANSLATE

Try to translate the words and phrases below into Chinese without looking at the list above.

1. robot

    ✎_____

2. GPS

    ✎_____

3. drone

    ✎_____

4. message

   ✎ _____

5. high-speed train

   ✎ _____

EXERCISE 2 - WHAT'S MISSING?

1. Take another look at five words and phrases in the following list:

   高铁
   网约车
   电动汽车
   无人驾驶
   无人机

   Now, cover up the list above with your hand or a piece of paper and complete the list below with the one that's missing.

   网约车
   电动汽车
   无人驾驶
   无人机

   ✎ _____

2. Let's do the same with another five words or phrases from the list:

   导航
   网上购物
   网上点餐
   亚马逊
   快递

Now, cover them up and spot what's missing from the list below:

快递
导航
网上购物
网上点餐

3. Here are the next five:

支付宝
扫码
人工智能
脑机对接
人脸识别

Which one is missing from the following list?

脑机对接
人脸识别
支付宝
扫码

4. Here is the final list of five pieces of vocabulary:

机器人
谷歌
脸书
微信
短信

Cover them up and fill in the gap with the missing word or phrase.

谷歌

脸书

机器人

短信

✎_____

EXERCISE 3 - ODD ONE OUT

1. Which *two* of the words or phrases from the list below would you be unlikely to use when talking about transportation?

网约车

无人驾驶

脑机对接

高铁

支付宝

✎_____

✎_____

2. Which *three* of the following words would you be unlikely to use when talking about communication?

短信

无人机

人脸识别

微信

高铁

✎_____

✎_____

✎_____

EXERCISE 4 - FILL IN THE GAPS

Fill in each gap with the most appropriate word from the vocabulary list. If you need to, you can refer to the list to help you.

1. 我有什么问题都会问 ✎_____ 。
   Wǒ yǒu shénme wèntí dōu huì wèn
   ✎_____ .

2. 将来 ✎_____ 可以给你送东西，
   不用人来。 **Jiānglái** ✎_____ **kěyǐ**
   gěi nǐ sòng dōngxi, bú yòng rén lái.

3. 自从有了 ✎_____ , 哥哥开车再
   也不迷路了。 **Zìcóng yǒule** ✎_____ ,
   gēge kāichē zàiyě bù mílù le.

4. ✎_____ 比传统汽车更加保护
   环境。 ✎_____ **bǐ chuántǒng**
   qìchē gèngjiā bǎohù huánjìng.

5. 将来 ✎_____ 会不会比我们人
   类更聪明? **Jiānglái** ✎_____
   huì bú huì bǐ wǒmen rénlèi gèng cōngming?

* * *

When you're ready, turn to pages 252-253 to find the answers to the exercises.

怎么用"把"
Zěnme yòng "bǎ"
GRAMMAR FOCUS

In this grammar activity, we are looking at the 把 **bǎ** construction – the most unique feature of Chinese grammar when compared to English. Read the short explanation below, then have a go at the three exercises that follow. 加油! **Jiāyóu!**

* * *

The 把 **bǎ** construction is one that many learners of Chinese find difficult. This is because some sentences could be grammatically correct both with and without 把 **bǎ**, but which one you use will depend on the context. It can also be tricky because the impact of using 把 **bǎ** in a sentence is often a change in emphasis, rather than an obvious change in meaning. So, in this activity we're going to practise understanding the difference between sentences that use 把 **bǎ** and sentences that don't, and see the contexts in which 把 **bǎ** may be used. First, let's look at these two sentences:

A. 玛丽写了一本书。 **Mǎlì xiě le yì běn shū.**
B. 玛丽把书写完了。 **Mǎlì bǎ shū xiě wán le.**

As you can see, sentence A follows the straightforward, standard structure of: *subject* (玛丽) + *verb* (写了) + *object* (一本书).

Sentence B, however, follows a different structure: *subject* + 把 **bǎ** + *object* + *verb*.

Both sentence A and sentence B tell us that Mary did something, but sentence A simply means *Mary wrote a book* while sentence B emphasises that Mary wrote this specific book and the job is done. Sentence A could be the answer to a question like *what did Mary do this summer?*, while sentence B could be the answer to *who wrote that book?* So, while the emphasis of sentence A is on Mary, the emphasis of sentence B is on the book. Also note that in 把 **bǎ** sentences the object has already been established or talked about (in this case, we already know from the question the book that we're talking about).

Compared with sentence A, sentence B with 把 **bǎ** makes two points:

1. The object is definite. We know which book Mary wrote.
2. The subject (Mary) caused a change to the definite object. The outcome is that this specific job is done.

Let's compare two more examples to see how 把 **bǎ** works:

C. **Jìrán Mǎlì zuò wǔfàn le, yídìng hěn lèi le. Wǒ lái zuò wǎnfàn ba.**

既然玛丽做午饭了，一定很累了。我来做晚饭吧。

D. **Jìrán Mǎlì bǎ wǔfàn zuòhǎo le, nà wǒmen xiànzài jiù chī ba.**

既然玛丽把午饭做好了，那我们现在就吃吧。

Like in sentence A, the emphasis of sentence C is also the subject, Mary. She prepared lunch and she is tired, so I will be the one to prepare dinner instead.

Like in sentence B, the emphasis of sentence D is the object. Lunch is ready, so we can eat anytime.

To summarise, the 把 **bǎ** construction places the emphasis of the sentence on the object, meaning that you'll tend to see 把 **bǎ** used in contexts where the object has been affected or changed in some way as a result of the action. Don't worry if you're sometimes unsure when to use 把 **bǎ** in your own sentences – the first step is to pay attention to when you see or hear other people using it and use the information above to consider why it has been used.

Now it's time to practise using the 把 **bǎ** structure in some exercises.

EXERCISE 1 - A BETTER TRANSLATION

Read the English sentence and decide if sentence A or sentence B is a better translation by circling the letter.

1. *I finished reading that book but still don't understand it.*
   A. 我看完那本书了，可是还是不懂。
   B. 我把那本书看完了，可是还是不懂。

2. *Mike gave the pen that he had just bought to Mary.*
   A. 麦克送给玛丽他刚刚买的笔了。
   B. 麦克把刚刚买的笔送给玛丽了。

3. *You have to finish the food you bought.*
   A. 你得把你买的饭吃完。
   B. 你得吃完你买的饭。

EXERCISE 2 - TRANSFORM USING 把 bǎ

Change the following into 把 **bǎ** sentences.

1. 她看完那个电影了。 **Tā kànwán nà ge diànyǐng le.**

    ✎_____

    _____

2. 妈妈做好饭了。 **Māma zuòhǎo fàn le.**

    ✎_____

    _____

3. 狗吃了猫的晚饭。 **Gǒu chī le māo de wǎnfàn.**

    ✎_____

    _____

EXERCISE 3 - COMPLETE THE DIALOGUES

Use 把 **bǎ** to complete the following dialogues, based on the English responses provided. Write in characters or in pinyin.

1. A. 麦克，我把你的箱子放哪里？ **Màikè, wǒ bǎ nǐ de xiāngzi fàng nǎlǐ?**

    B. ✎_____

    _____

    Please put my suitcase over there.

2. A. 爸爸，我的电脑到哪里去了？**Bàba, wǒ de diànnǎo dào nǎlǐ qù le?**

   B. ✎ _____

   _____

   I put your computer inside the suitcase.

3. A. 姐姐，我们现在去打篮球吧。 **Jiějie, wǒmen xiànzài qù dǎ lánqiú ba.**

   B. ✎ _____

   _____

   Finish your homework before we go and play basketball.

* * *

Turn to page 254 to check your answers.

41. 乒乓球 Pīngpāngqiú
READING FOCUS

EXERCISE 1 - COMPREHENSION

1. Yes, table tennis can be played in doubles.

2. 11 points.

3. When the returned ball does not fall on your side of the table, you win one point.

4. The sides alternate, each serving twice.

5. They need to keep playing until one side wins two points over the other.

EXERCISE 2 - TRANSLATE

1. tennis

2. sports, exercise

3. team event

4. to rotate, to take turns

5. to win

EXERCISE 3 - FIND THE CHINESE

1. 发球 fāqiú

2. 单打 dāndǎ

3. 五局三胜 wǔ jú sān shèng

4. 得一分 dé yì fēn

5. 打一局 dǎ yì jú

42. 怎么用"的、地、得" Zěnme yòng "dè, dì, dé"
GRAMMAR FOCUS

1. 妹妹**的**书包很小。 Mèimei de shūbāo hěn xiǎo.

   TRANSLATION: *My younger sister's backpack is very small.*

2. 她很快**地**就把书还给了我。 Tā hěn kuài de jiù bǎ shū huángěi le wǒ.

   TRANSLATION: *She quickly returned the book to me.*

3. 姐姐写英文写**得**很快，可是写汉字写**得**很慢。 Jiějie xiě Yīngwén xiě de hěn kuài, kěshì xiě Hànzì xiě de hěn màn.

   TRANSLATION: *My older sister writes in English very fast, but she writes in Chinese very slowly.*

4. 我累**得**站不起来了。 Wǒ lèi de zhàn bù qǐlái le.

   TRANSLATION: *I am so tired that I can't stand up.*

5. 妈妈给我做的衣服总是太大。 **Māma gěi wǒ zuò de yīfu zǒngshì tài dà.**

TRANSLATION: *The clothes that my mother made for me were always too big.*

6. 最好的大学不一定最贵。 **Zuìhǎo de dàxué bù yídìng zuì guì.**

TRANSLATION: *The best university is not necessarily the most expensive.*

7. 你拉什么乐器拉得最好? **Nǐ lā shénme yuèqì lā de zuìhǎo.**

TRANSLATION: *Which musical instrument do you play best?*

8. 弟弟慢慢地拿出来了他的手机。 **Dìdi mànmàn de ná chūlái le tā de shǒujī.**

TRANSLATION: *My younger brother slowly took out his mobile phone.*

9. 我在这里吃得很好, 玩得也很好。 **Wǒ zài zhèlǐ chī de hěn hǎo, wán de yě hěn hǎo.**

TRANSLATION: *I eat well and have a good time here.*

10. 姐姐忙得没有时间吃饭。 **Jiějie máng de méi yǒu shíjiān chīfàn.**

TRANSLATION: *My older sister is so busy that she has no time for meals.*

43. 旅行 Lǚxíng
VOCABULARY CONSOLIDATION

EXERCISE 1 - TRANSLATE

1. 行程 xíngchéng
2. 度假 dùjià
3. 旅行社 lǚxíngshè

4. 迷路 mílù

5. 打行李 dǎ xíngli

EXERCISE 2 - WHAT'S MISSING?

1. 到达 dàodá – *to arrive*

2. 观景 guānjǐng – *sightseeing*

3. 乘邮船 chéng yóuchuán – *to go on a cruise*

4. 出差 chūchāi – *to go on a business trip*

EXERCISE 3 - ODD ONE OUT

1. 乘邮船 chéng yóuchuán – *to go on a cruise*

   旅游问讯处 lǚyóu wènxùnchù – *tourist information office*

2. 时差 shíchā – *time difference*

   大使馆 dàshǐguǎn – *embassy*

   护照 hùzhào – *passport*

EXERCISE 4 - FILL IN THE GAPS

1. 去一个国家旅游之前，要先去那个国家的大使馆**申请签证**。 Qù yí ge guójiā lǚyóu zhīqián, yào xiān qù nàge guójiā de dàshǐguǎn **shēnqǐng qiānzhèng**.

   TRANSLATION: *Before travelling to a foreign country, you need to go to that country's embassy to apply for a visa.*

2. 北京和纽约的**时差**是几个小时？ Běijīng hé Niǔyuē de **shíchā** shì jǐ ge xiǎoshí?

   TRANSLATION: *What is the time difference between Beijing and New York?*

3. 出去旅行，我喜欢**住酒店**，不喜欢住在朋友家里。
Chūqù lǚxíng, wǒ xǐhuan **zhù jiǔdiàn**, bù xǐhuan zhù zài péngyou jiālǐ.
TRANSLATION: *When I travel, I like to stay in a hotel, I don't like to stay at a friend's house.*

4. 上飞机的时候，一定要出示**登机牌**。 Shàng fēijī de shíhou, yídìng yào chūshì **dēngjīpái**.
TRANSLATION: *When you board an aeroplane, you need to show your boarding pass.*

5. 应该离开酒店出发了，可是我还没有**打行李**。
Yīnggāi líkāi jiǔdiàn chūfā le, kěshì wǒ hái méi yǒu **dǎ xíngli**.
TRANSLATION: *We should leave the hotel now, but I haven't packed yet.*

44. 我的朋友李萌 Wǒ de péngyou Lǐ Méng
READING FOCUS

EXERCISE 1 - COMPREHENSION

1. She is an engineer.
2. Black.
3. She likes to wear western suits and jeans.
4. She likes to eat vegetables, fruits, fish and shrimp. She doesn't like to eat meat.
5. She likes to play table tennis and swim.
6. She has travelled to Asia, Africa and South America.

45. 比较 Bǐjiào
GRAMMAR FOCUS

EXERCISE 1 - CREATE COMPARISONS

1. 我的裙子比你的裙子贵十美元。 **Wǒ de qúnzi bǐ nǐ de qúnzi guì shí měiyuán.**

   TRANSLATION: *My skirt is $10 more expensive than your skirt.*

2. 妹妹比姐姐跑得快。 **Mèimei bǐ jiějie pǎo de kuài.**

   TRANSLATION: *My younger sister runs faster than my older sister.*

3. 麦克比李明高一尺。 **Màikè bǐ Lǐ Míng gāo yì chǐ.**

   TRANSLATION: *Mike is one foot taller than Li Ming.*

4. 我写英文比我写汉字写得漂亮。 **Wǒ xiě Yīngwén bǐ wǒ xiě Hànzì xiě de piàoliang.**

   TRANSLATION: *I write English more beautifully than I write Chinese characters.*

EXERCISE 2 - Q&A

1. 我爸爸比我妈妈高三寸。 **Wǒ bàba bǐ wǒ māma gāo sān cùn.**

   TRANSLATION: *My father is three inches taller than my mother.*

2. 妈妈做饭比爸爸做饭做得好很多。 **Māma zuòfàn bǐ bàba zuòfàn zuò de hǎo hěn duō.**

   TRANSLATION: *My mother cooks much better than my father.*

3. 我跳舞没有/不如我妹妹跳舞跳得好。 **Wǒ tiàowǔ méi yǒu / búrù wǒ mèimei tiàowǔ tiào de hǎo.**
or 我没有/不如我妹妹跳舞跳得好。 **Wǒ méi yǒu / búrù wǒ mèimei tiàowǔ tiào de hǎo.**

TRANSLATION: *I don't dance as well as my sister.*

4. 英语没有汉语难学。 **Yīngyǔ méi yǒu Hànyǔ nán xué.**
or 英语不如汉语难学。 **Yīngyǔ bùrú Hànyǔ nán xué.**

TRANSLATION: *English is not as difficult to learn as Chinese.*

5. 明天的天气没有今天的天气好。 **Míngtiān de tiānqì méi yǒu jīntiān de tiānqì hǎo.**
or 明天的天气不如今天的天气好。 **Míngtiān de tiānqì bùrú jīntiān de tiānqì hǎo.**

TRANSLATION: *The weather tomorrow will not be as good as today's weather.*

46. 音乐 Yīnyuè
VOCABULARY CONSOLIDATION

EXERCISE 1 - TRANSLATE

1. 唱歌 chànggē
2. 拉小提琴 lā xiǎotíqín
3. 吹法国号 chuī fǎguóhào
4. 弹钢琴 tán gāngqín
5. 打铃 dǎlíng

EXERCISE 2 - WHAT'S MISSING?

1. 拉小提琴 lā xiǎotíqín – *to play the violin*
2. 打锣 dǎluó – *to play the gong*

3. 弹琵琶 tán pípá – *to play pipa*

4. 唱京剧 chàng jīngjù – *to sing Beijing opera*

EXERCISE 3 - FILL IN THE GAPS

1. 她的爸爸喜欢管乐，他会吹法国号/唢呐/口琴/笛子。Tā de bàba xǐhuan guǎnyuè, tā huì **chuī fǎguóhào / suǒnà / kǒuqín / dízi**.

    TRANSLATION: *Her father likes to play wind instruments. He can play the French horn / suona / harmonica / flute.*

2. 她的妈妈喜欢弦乐，她会拉小提琴/中提琴/大提琴/二胡。Tā de māma xǐhuan xiányuè, tā huì **lā xiǎotíqín / zhōngtíqín / dàtíqín / èrhú**.

    TRANSLATION: *Her mother likes to play string instruments. She can play the violin / viola / cello / erhu.*

3. 她的姐姐喜欢弹拨乐，她会弹钢琴/吉他/琵琶/电子琴。Tā de jiějie xǐhuan tánbōyuè, tā huì **tán gāngqín / jítā / pípá / diànzǐqín**.

    TRANSLATION: *Her older sister likes to play keyboard and plucked instruments. She can play the piano / guitar / pipa / keyboard.*

4. 她的哥哥喜欢打击乐，他会打鼓/打锣/打镲/打铃。Tā de gēge xǐhuan dǎjīyuè, tā huì **dǎ gǔ / dǎ luó / dǎ chǎ / dǎ líng**.

    TRANSLATION: *Her older brother likes to play percussion. He can play the drums / gong / cymbals / bells.*

5. 她很喜欢唱歌，还会唱民歌/歌剧/京剧。Tā hěn xǐhuan chànggē, hái huì **chàng míngē / gējù / jīngjù**.

    TRANSLATION: *She really likes singing. She can also sing folk songs / opera / Beijing opera.*

47. 中国城 Zhōngguóchéng
READING FOCUS

1. 有人的地方就会有中国人。 **Yǒurén de dìfāng jiù huì yǒu Zhōngguórén.**

TRANSLATION: *Wherever there are people, there are Chinese people.*

2. 一般都有中国城。 **Yībān dōu yǒu zhōngguóchéng.**

TRANSLATION: *Most cities have a Chinatown.*

3. 不一样大。有的大, 有的小。 **Bù yíyàng dà. Yǒude dà, yǒude xiǎo.**

TRANSLATION: *They are not all the same size. Some are big, some are small.*

4. 不在市中心, 但是离市中心不太远。 **Bùzài shìzhōngxīn, dànshì lí shìzhōngxīn bú tài yuǎn.**

TRANSLATION: *It isn't usually in the city centre, but not too far from the city centre.*

5. 中国城不是一个城堡, 而是几条街。 **Zhōngguóchéng bùshì yí ge chéngbǎo, érshì jǐ tiáo jiē.**

TRANSLATION: *Chinatown is not a castle, but a few streets.*

6. 有商店、中餐馆、中药店、各种会馆和中文学校。 **Yǒu shāngdiàn, zhōngcānguǎn, zhōngyàodiàn, gèzhǒng huìguǎn hé Zhōngwén xuéxiào.**

TRANSLATION: *There are shops, Chinese restaurants, Chinese medicine stores, various associations and Chinese schools.*

7. 他们游行。 有舞狮, 舞龙的队伍。 **Tāmen yóuxíng. Yǒu wǔshī, wǔlóng de duìwǔ.**

TRANSLATION: *They have parades. There are lion and dragon dance teams.*

8. 我也要对别人说"恭喜发财"。 **Wǒ yě yào duì biérén shuō "gōngxǐ fācái".**

TRANSLATION: *I also wish you prosperity.*

48. 怎么用"被" Zěnme yòng "bèi"
GRAMMAR FOCUS

EXERCISE 1 - TRANSFORM

1. 电视被弟弟不小心打坏了。 **Diànshì bèi dìdi bù xiǎoxīn dǎ huài le.**

TRANSLATION: *The TV has been broken accidentally by my younger brother.*

2. 我的房间被妹妹整理好了。 **Wǒ de fángjiān bèi mèimei zhěnglǐ hǎo le.**

TRANSLATION: *My room has been tidied up by my younger sister.*

3. 我的书包被偷走了。 **Wǒ de shūbāo bèi tōu zǒu le.**

TRANSLATION: *My backpack has been stolen.*

4. 她被朋友请去吃饭了。 **Tā bèi péngyou qǐng qù chīfàn le.**

TRANSLATION: *She has been invited to dinner by her friends.*

EXERCISE 2 - Q&A

1. 你的书被你的妹妹拿走了。 **Nǐ de shū bèi nǐ de mèimei ná zǒu le.**

TRANSLATION: *Your book was taken away by your younger sister.*

2. 我的新手机被偷走了。 **Wǒ de xīn shǒujī bèi tōu zǒu le.**

TRANSLATION: *My new phone was stolen.*

3. 我的车被女儿开走了。 **Wǒ de chē bèi nǔ'ér kāi zǒu le.**

TRANSLATION: *My car was driven away by my daughter.*

4. 这本书非常好，被翻译成很多种语言了。 **Zhè běn shū fēicháng hǎo, bèi fānyì chéng hěn duō zhǒng yǔyán le.**

TRANSLATION: *This book is very good. It has been translated into many languages.*

5. 她被我们老师表扬了几句。 **Tā bèi wǒmen lǎoshī biǎoyáng le jǐ jù.**

TRANSLATION: *She was praised by our teacher.*

49. 新科技 Xīn kējì
VOCABULARY CONSOLIDATION

EXERCISE 1 - TRANSLATE

1. 机器人 jīqìrén
2. 导航 dǎoháng
3. 无人机 wúrénjī
4. 短信 duǎnxìn
5. 高铁 gāotiě

EXERCISE 2 - WHAT'S MISSING?

1. 高铁 gāotiě – *high-speed train*
2. 亚马逊 Yàmǎxùn – *Amazon*
3. 人工智能 réngōng zhìnéng – *artificial intelligence*
4. 微信 Wēixìn – *WeChat*

EXERCISE 3 - ODD ONE OUT

1. 脑机对接 **nǎojī duìjiē** – *brain-computer interface*
   支付宝 **Zhīfùbǎo** – *Alipay*

2. 无人机 **wúrénjī** – *drone*
   人脸识别 **rénliǎn shíbié** – *facial recognition*
   高铁 **gāotiě** – *high-speed train*

EXERCISE 4 - FILL IN THE GAPS

1. 我有什么问题都会问**谷歌**。 Wǒ yǒu shénme wèntí
   dōu huì wèn **Gǔgē**.

   TRANSLATION: *I always ask Google any questions I have.*

2. 将来**无人机**可以给你送东西，不用人来。
   Jiānglái **wúrénjī** kěyǐ gěi nǐ sòng dōngxi, bú yòng rén lái.

   TRANSLATION: *In the future, drones will be able to deliver things to
   you without the need for humans.*

3. 自从有了**导航**，哥哥开车再也不迷路了。
   Zìcóng yǒule **dǎoháng**, gēge kāichē zàiyě bù mílù le.

   TRANSLATION: *Since he got a GPS, my older brother has never got lost
   while driving.*

4. **电动汽车**比传统汽车更加保护环境。 **Diàndòng
   qìchē** bǐ chuántǒng qìchē gèngjiā bǎohù huánjìng.

   TRANSLATION: *Electric cars are better for the environment than
   traditional cars.*

5. 将来**人工智能**会不会比我们人类更聪明？
   Jiānglái **réngōng zhìnéng** huì bú huì bǐ wǒmen rénlèi gèng
   cōngming?

   TRANSLATION: *Will AI be smarter than us humans in the future?*

50. 怎么用"把" Zěnme yòng "bǎ"
GRAMMAR FOCUS

EXERCISE 1 - A BETTER TRANSLATION

1. B. 我把那本书看完了，可是还是不懂。 **Wǒ bǎ nà běn shū kàn wán le, kěshì háishi bù dǒng.**

2. B. 麦克把刚刚买的笔送给玛丽了。 **Màikè bǎ gānggāng mǎi de bǐ sònggěi Mǎlì le.**

3. A. 你得把你买的饭吃完。 **Nǐ déi bǎ nǐ mǎi de fàn chīwán.**

EXERCISE 2 - TRANSFORM USING 把 bǎ

1. 她把那个电影看完了。 **Tā bǎ nà ge diànyǐng kàn wán le.**
   TRANSLATION: *She finished watching that movie.*

2. 妈妈把饭做好了。 **Māma bǎ fàn zuò hǎo le.**
   TRANSLATION: *Mum got the meal ready.*

3. 狗把猫的晚饭吃了。 **Gǒu bǎ māo de wǎnfàn chī le.**
   TRANSLATION: *The dog ate the cat's dinner.*

EXERCISE 3 - COMPLETE THE DIALOGUES

1. 请把我的箱子放在那里。 **Qǐng bǎ wǒ de xiāngzi fàng zài nàlǐ.**
   TRANSLATION: *Please put my suitcase over there.*

2. 我把你的电脑放到箱子里了。 **Wǒ bǎ nǐ de diànnǎo fàng dào xiāngzi lǐ le.**
   TRANSLATION: *I put your computer inside the suitcase.*

3. 你先把作业做完我们再去打篮球。 **Nǐ xiān bǎ zuòyè zuòwán wǒmen zài qù dǎ lánqiú.**
   TRANSLATION: *Finish your homework before we go and play basketball.*

ACKNOWLEDGEMENTS

This book has very much been a team effort and I would like to take the opportunity to thank the people who have helped to put it together.

Firstly, thanks to Meaghan Lim, Claire Lipscomb and the whole team at Teach Yourself. It's been a pleasure to work with you all and we'd like to thank you for your belief in the project and your enthusiasm for helping us bring Coffee Break to a new audience around the world.

谢谢 **xièxie** Licheng Gu, who has brought his huge experience in teaching Chinese to learners around the world to the development of the activities in this book, helping you to practise and improve your Chinese in a fun and effective way.

We'd also like to thank Ana Belén Enríquez Cambón for contributing her perspective as a learner of Chinese.

Thank you Ava Dinwoodie, our Series Editor, whose dedication to the project and expert coordination meant that everyone knew exactly what they were doing and when it needed to be done!

Finally, thank you for reading the book and we very much hope you have enjoyed building your skills in Chinese with us.

You may recall my mention of jazz virtuoso Charlie Parker in the Introduction to this book, who, by focusing on practice, practice, practice, was then ready to fly and enjoy his performance. I hope that you're now feeling ready to let go and incorporate the new vocabulary, expressions and grammatical structures into your Chinese on a daily basis.

Mark Pentleton - Founder, Coffee Break Languages

SHARE YOUR THOUGHTS

If you'd like to help other learners like yourself discover Coffee Break Chinese, we'd be very grateful if you would consider leaving an honest review. If you bought the book online, you can do this easily by going to the website where you found it.

谢谢! **Xièxie!** Thank you for sharing your thoughts and for helping other learners practise their Chinese on their Coffee Break.

NOTES

RAISING READERS
Books Build Bright Futures

Dear Reader,

We'd love your attention for one more page to tell you about the crisis in children's reading, and what we can all do.

Studies have shown that reading for fun is the **single biggest predictor of a child's future life chances** – more than family circumstance, parents' educational background or income. It improves academic results, mental health, wealth, communication skills, ambition and happiness.[1]

The number of children reading for fun is in rapid decline. Young people have a lot of competition for their time. In 2024, 1 in 10 children and young people in the UK aged 5 to 18 did not own a single book at home.[2]

Hachette works extensively with schools, libraries and literacy charities, but here are some ways we can all raise more readers:

- Reading to children for just 10 minutes a day makes a difference
- Don't give up if children aren't regular readers – there will be books for them!
- Visit bookshops and libraries to get recommendations
- Encourage them to listen to audiobooks
- Support school libraries
- Give books as gifts

There's a lot more information about how to encourage children to read on our website: **www.RaisingReaders.co.uk**

Thank you for reading.

hachette
UK

---

[1] OECD, '21st-Century Readers: Developing Literacy Skills in a Digital World', 2021, https://www.oecd.org/en/publications/21st-century-readers_a83d84cb-en.html

[2] National Literacy Trust, 'Book Ownership in 2024', November 2024, https://literacytrust.org.uk/research-services/research-reports/book-ownership-in-2024

ALSO BY COFFEE BREAK LANGUAGES

Are you also learning another language? Or do you have a friend or relative who's a learner of a different language? Our *50 Coffee Breaks* series also includes books in English, French, Italian, German, Swedish, Scottish Gaelic and Spanish, available both in paperback and as ebooks.

Just visit fiftycoffeebreaks.com.

See you soon, à bientôt, a presto, bis bald, vi ses, chì sinn a dh'aithghearr thu and ¡hasta pronto!

MORE COFFEE BREAK LEARNING

Here at Coffee Break Languages we provide learning through podcasts, courses, videos and books. For more learning from Coffee Break, just visit:

coffeebreaklanguages.com/chinese

Find us on your favourite social media platform by searching for Coffee Break Languages.

再见! Zàijiàn!

f facebook.com/coffeebreaklanguages

X x.com/coffeebreaklang

◎ instagram.com/coffeebreaklanguages

▶ youtube.com/@coffeebreaklanguages